THE NEWS
IS READ

THE NEWS IS READ

—BY—

CHARLOTTE GREEN

The Robson Press

First published in Great Britain in 2014 by
The Robson Press (an imprint of Biteback Publishing Ltd)
Westminster Tower
3 Albert Embankment
London SE1 7SP

ISBN 978-1-84954-691-1

10 9 8 7 6 5 4 3 2 1

A CIP catalogue record for this book is available from the British Library.

Set in Fournier

Printed and bound in Great Britain by
CPI Group (UK) Ltd, Croydon CR0 4YY

For my parents, Ruth and Geoffrey,
in memoriam, and for my sister, Rachel

CONTENTS

'While thou livest keep a good tongue in thy head'

— THE TEMPEST, ACT III, SCENE II

Chapter 1

THE LAST DAY

18 JANUARY 2013: my final day in the BBC newsroom after twenty-seven years as a newsreader and continuity announcer on Radio 4. And thirty-four years in total at this often infuriating but always lovable institution. In other words, a BBC 'lifer'.

When I woke up that morning and opened the curtains, snow had fallen during the night enveloping everything and bestowing a strange, muffled calm on the neighbourhood. The garden looked beautiful under its pristine covering; a squirrel scuttled up the large fir tree at the back of the house. I worried momentarily that my friends wouldn't be able to make it into London that evening to help me celebrate, but a series of texts reassured me. 'Nothing's going to stop us getting in'; 'we'll be there – it's only snow'. My friends are intrepid and inventive so I knew that the prospect of good food and wine, as well as fun and laughter, would entice them in, whatever the weather.

I trudged to the station through the snow, now rapidly turning to a filthy brown slush – I had no difficulty getting in to Oxford Circus. It felt slightly odd, but at the same time uplifting, knowing that this would be the last time I did this journey as a commuter. The feeling of doing everything for the last time recurred throughout the day like a musical leitmotif – last 11 a.m. summary, last appearance on *WATO* (*The World at One*), last afternoon briefing meeting and last 6 p.m. bulletin. There was a small element of sadness, but primarily I felt excited about the future and the myriad possibilities that it held.

My hopes of keeping a low profile throughout the day came to nothing when David Sillito, the BBC arts correspondent, came up to my desk in the newsroom and politely asked if he could interview me for the one o'clock TV news bulletin. I'm fundamentally quite shy – in spite of my feeling of ease and confidence at the microphone, I don't feel comfortable in front of a camera, so was very reluctant to agree. David, however, was silkily persistent – and looking back now, I'm very glad that he was. He put together a lovely piece, which paid tribute to my career at the BBC. I felt a great deal of pride that TV was honouring someone so steeped in radio. The night before, *Newsnight* had broadcast their own appreciation, which was affectionate and jokey. I also read out their end credits, which had been especially written for me. I was introduced by Kirsty Wark as Radio 4 royalty, who for some bizarre reason had been allowed to hang up her crown. A deliberate note of scepticism was introduced in the credits – a radio veteran jokily scoffing at the professional capabilities of a television production team. I began by reading out '*Newsnight* was presented by Kirsty Wark – well, she's blanked me in the canteen before now!', and ended by saying incredulously '*Newsnight*! I was booked to do *Holby City*. I'd never have come on if there'd been the slightest suggestion I'd end up on (beep to obscure rude word) *Newsnight*.' By this point my voice was dripping with vitriol and I was relishing the opportunity to camp it up a bit. Incidentally, I was delighted when just over a year later, Kirsty Wark was a guest on my *Culture Club* programme on Classic FM. She came in to discuss her debut novel, *The Legacy of Elizabeth Pringle*, and afterwards, off air, we happily talked shop about the BBC and the joys and frustrations of working there.

Throughout the day, the awareness of a large and very important part of my life drawing to an end became acute, heightened by people I'd never met before greeting me at my desk or in the lift, thanking me and saying how much my voice would be missed. One man told me that it had been the backdrop to his life ever since I had started in the mid-1980s. It's overwhelming when people, particularly strangers, tell you these things, not least because of their obvious sincerity and kindness. Similarly, my inbox never stopped pinging with heartfelt, thoughtful and frankly inspiring words from friends, colleagues and listeners. It began to feel unreal, as if I was starring in a feel-good film with James Stewart hovering nearby, ready to step in and tell me how good life was and how it should be cherished.

Six o'clock drew near and soon I'd be reading my final news bulletin. I felt utterly calm throughout the programme, an acceptance that this was the culmination of my career as a newsreader. The newsroom journalists made one final attempt to get me to giggle on air, naughtily including a story about the American tennis player 'Gorgeous' Gussie Moran and the frilly pants she wore at Wimbledon in the 1940s!

I said my last ever 'BBC News' and friends and family sitting in the studio control room, who had watched the bulletin go out, all cheered and whooped with delight. Photos were taken and then I walked back to the newsroom feeling a mixture of elation, relief and wistfulness. It's a cliché, but what happened next will stay with me for the rest of my life.

As I made my way back to my desk everybody in the newsroom stood and applauded, those working for television as well as radio. It continued for a long time after I reached the six o'clock bulletin desk; and it was spontaneous, heartfelt and deeply moving. People stood everywhere – lining the spiral staircase and up in the gallery, many of them unknown to me, yet all taking the time to pay me a wonderful compliment and give me a memorable send-off. It was utterly overwhelming and my determination not to get tearful dissolved within moments. I caught sight of my sister who looked immensely proud, which made me cry a little bit more. I wished my parents were still alive and could have been there with me; we had been a very close, loving family and they would have loved the occasion, particularly the chance to talk to my friends and colleagues.

Juliet, a close friend of mine with whom I've shared a lot of laughter over the years, executed the most perfect piercing whistle and everybody laughed. Helen Boaden, then the director of BBC News, stepped forward, gave me a big hug and thrust a glass of champagne into my hand. The party had begun!

Richard Clarke, the head of the newsroom, gave a very generous and funny speech and I replied off the top of my head, having forgotten to prepare anything earlier in the day. I received some lovely presents – including a much-cherished Spurs scarf! – and some beautiful cards, quite a few of them rude (everyone in the newsroom was familiar with my bawdy sense of humour!). My colleague Diana Speed kindly gave me a huge sheaf of complimentary tweets and comments on the BBC log that she had printed off.

After lots of hugs and more tears, my sister, close friends and I set off for supper in my favourite bistro. It had stopped snowing, but snow still carpeted the roads and pavements. We all piled into taxis, talking excitedly and looking forward to an evening full of fun, with plenty of good food and wine. The evening passed in a blur of happy reminiscence and funny stories, which inevitably got ruder as the evening progressed. Eventually our stomachs were aching with laughter and our voices grew hoarse from talking and laughing so much. At one point I sat back in my chair and watched the rest of the party, wanting to capture and distil the moment in my mind and memory. If I could, I would have made time stand still; I felt in that moment I couldn't possibly be happier or more content. Someone soon put their arm round me and brought me back into the lively conversation around the table and the moment that I wanted to hold onto forever inevitably passed, as it had to. Reflection and thought could wait for another day.

Nobody wanted to go home after the meal so we piled into a friend's flat across the road. There were more drinks and even more laughter and silliness. We ended up with loo rolls on our heads – don't ask! – and I had my Spurs scarf ceremoniously wrapped round my neck. Eventually, the revelry came to an end and the party reluctantly broke up. It was the early hours of the next day, snow had started to fall again and it crunched softly under our feet. The whole evening had been the perfect end to an extraordinary day.

I had come to the end of a remarkably satisfying and – for the most part – immensely happy career at the BBC, and was looking forward excitedly to new and very different challenges. But now I want to look back, to the events and circumstances that set me on the path that ultimately led to my unforgettable final day and farewell.

Chapter 2

'CREEPING LIKE A SNAIL UNWILLINGLY TO SCHOOL'

AT THE AGE of four I went to a small local prep school, St Aidan's. There's a photo of me in school uniform taken at the time, with my Panama hat at a jaunty angle on my head and my hair tied in bunches. Lance, an unpleasant boy in my class who was always sneaking up on the girls, had tried many times to untie the red ribbon that held them in shape, as an act of sabotage. Unable to re-tie the ribbon, I would wander around all day at school with one bunch rather than two, looking rather lopsided.

When I first started there I used to be in floods of tears in the morning before leaving home. I'd obviously been having far too good a time with my mother and perhaps didn't like the change in routine. I would cling onto a chair or any handily placed piece of furniture, to stop myself being put in the car for the journey to school. Once there my attention was diverted, I'd become absorbed in an activity and the tears would stop. I remember one of my best friends at the time, Anthony, also being dragged unwillingly down the path leading to the school, equally reluctant to go in. He kept being put in the corner during Assembly because he couldn't resist stroking my hair, which was very blonde and soft. He also liked to stroke my mother's hair, which was similarly fine but auburn, as he stood behind her while she drove the car to school – she and Anthony's mother Jean shared the school run. This was in the days before children's car seats and seat belts. Throughout his early childhood he always referred to her 'organ' hair and often called her 'Aunty Roof', unable to pronounce Ruth. My other memory of St Aidan's is of sitting at a splintery wooden desk in the back row of the class next to Richard, who had blonde hair, dark eyes and long, dark eyelashes. He was a gentle boy, less rumbustious than the others in the class and inclined to dreaminess. We chatted away together a lot, often ignoring what was going on during the lesson.

There were more hot tears and entreaties to stay at home before the entrance test for Haberdashers' Aske's. My poor mother had another struggle to get me there, cajoling me into the school where I was met by one of the teachers. The staff knew me because my sister was already a pupil there. I was given the biggest sheet of paper I'd ever seen and asked to draw a picture of my house. I liked drawing and filled the entire sheet, adding endless detail and including our front and back garden. My father's wheelbarrow was there, as well as the swing. I became so engrossed I was actually the last to leave; my mother came looking for me and was astounded to find me with my head bent over the picture, oblivious to everything around me. The tears had been completely forgotten.

At about this time, I had an imaginary friend, Janet. She accompanied me in all my escapades, but if I did something naughty Janet was always to blame. My mother would play along with this and often asked how Janet was, and whether she would like a piece of cake or a glass of orange juice. I think I invented her because I was growing tired of being bossed about by my sister, Rachel, and being blamed whenever we got into trouble. Janet was my confidante, but was also a convenient scapegoat who would take the rap for my misdeeds. I happily chatted away to her in my head; she was someone to turn to when Rachel, four years older, grew tired of me and told me to go away. When she was in the mood,

Rachel would call me her villain-friend and we would have adventures together. This was fun, but sometimes marred by her demands that I fetch and carry for her! I used to be bribed with the offer of sixpence to go and get something for her from her bedroom. I would duti-fully trot off upstairs, bring back whatever was wanted and wait expectantly for my payment. I soon learned that the reward was never going to be forthcoming, and so headed off into the realms of my imagination with Janet, who never let me down.

My first school report when I was five stated that 'Charlotte has a voice like a fog-horn and must learn when it is appropriate to use it.' I loved to chatter and I couldn't understand why that had to stop when we were having lessons. I've always had a relatively deep, low voice which contrasted with the high, squeaky voice of Anthony, much to the amusement of our respective families. He would stand at the front door and ask in a piping voice if 'Chartot' could come out to play. My mother told me later that she would laugh to herself as we wandered off into the garden deep in conversation, Anthony squeaking away happily and me responding in a soft contralto.

I loved to read out loud from the papers when I was small, much to Rachel's annoyance. I would sit at the dining table while she would be at the piano, deliber-ately playing loudly in order to drown me out. It was a battle of wills and our mother always had to adjudicate over who had the right to stay in there and who had to leave the room. 'But I was here first' was the constant cry, and Ma – who was scrupulously fair – would tell us that we were like a couple of Kilkenny cats and should stop bickering with each other.

When I was seven years old, the Christine Keeler/John Profumo scandal was all over the papers. I remember reading the coverage out loud without having the faintest idea what it all meant and what the true ramifications were. I knew somehow that it was exciting and had a certain mystery attached to it. This was underlined when my parents discovered what I was doing and made strenuous efforts to hide the newspapers from me. At first I was intrigued and made equally vigorous attempts to discover where they were hidden, but soon grew bored and headed off into the garden to play or go on the swing. My sister and I would propel ourselves higher and higher until the swing's structure began to shake, and then launch ourselves off, aiming to land on a cushion set some way down the garden. Despite landing awkwardly on occasions, we never seemed to get hurt, nor did we break any limbs. I experienced pure joy on the rare instances when I landed plumb on the cushion.

My sister was mad about horses and being four years older than me usually dictated what games were played. She went through a phase of setting up gymkhanas in the garden, complete with miniature jumps and even a water-jump. This sounds grand but in reality consisted of the washing-up bowl filled with water. The jumps were Heath Robinson affairs, made up from old planks and oil cans plundered from the garage. Rachel naturally always had a clear round. To clarify, I should say that we were the horses and that the jumps were only about a foot off the ground. I always managed to have a clear round as well, but somehow Rachel would always maintain that there had been a minor infringement and I would be given four faults. I became increasingly disgruntled with these imaginary mistakes and would usually stomp off to do something else.

Our childhood was incredibly happy, full of laughter, teasing and fun. We were exceptionally fortunate to have kind, gentle and very loving parents who gave us both a wonderful start in life. They were never indulgent with us and so we managed to avoid becoming spoilt, demanding little monsters. They were clear-eyed about our faults and failings and were always firm on the occasions when we were told off. We grew up with a strong sense of right and wrong and were taught to treat others with respect and courtesy.

My sister and I attended Sunday school throughout our childhood. I'm afraid its essential message of salvation through Christ rather passed me by; I was much more interested in meeting my friends and having a good time. We sang choruses, listened to Bible readings and drew pictures depicting various Bible stories. My friend Jane and I extracted some fun from the situation by mimicking the conductor and being rude about the grown-ups. One or two of them seemed impossibly pious and holy and we did our best to keep out of their way. Unfortunately, we were once discovered finishing off the dregs of the Communion wine at the back of the church and were severely rebuked. Small children don't understand the concept of transubstantiation and merely see the chance to have a free drink. We thought it was Ribena so were a bit disappointed by the sour taste.

One year a small play was put on depicting the raising of Lazarus from the dead – not the most punchy or exciting story for small children to act out. I didn't take part that year but watched fascinated as my friend, Robert – who was playing Lazarus – stole the show. He lay on the floor under a table for some reason, supposedly dead. Robert, however, decided to make the most of his part and began rolling his eyes back into his head, fidgeting and even eating something that he'd found in his pocket! I thought this was wonderful and the audience began to laugh; emboldened by this response, Robert, reaching the point in the story where Lazarus is raised from the dead, leapt up and did a little jig. He then pulled an awful face, did a Bugs Bunny impression and ran off the stage. It was the stand-out moment of my entire Sunday school attendance.

There was always laughter in our family. Both my parents had a good sense of humour and saw the funny side to most things. They taught us to laugh at ourselves

and not take ourselves too seriously. We all found ribaldry and earthiness funny – and I, in particular, had an
obsession with bottoms and bodily functions. My friends
and I would all squeal with delight if bottoms came up
in conversation, even in the most innocuous way. On
one occasion during the school holidays my sister and I
went for a riding lesson; my pony was called Pooh after
Winnie the Pooh – which, given my fascination with all
things bottom-related, seemed highly appropriate. He
was a docile creature, content to crop the grass and amble
along at a steady pace, rather than break into a trot. I was
secretly pleased that Pooh was so compliant, having had
an unpleasant experience with Rosebud, a donkey on the
beach, earlier in the holiday. Her minder had whacked
her on the rump rather too enthusiastically and she shot
off at great speed over the wet sand. My saddle began to
slip and I ended up at 90 degrees to the rampant donkey,
clinging on desperately. Old cine footage shows my father
and the minder racing after Rosebud in a vain attempt
to catch up with her before I fell off. Falling face down
onto wet sand is not funny and I started to howl. Pa came
to the rescue and a large ice-cream with extra chocolate
flake went a long way to easing my bruised body and
hurt pride. I'd also been delighted, given my scatological bent, that Rosebud, once she had been stopped, did
a lengthy and very loud fart.

My parents were remarkably tolerant of burps and
farts, as long as they were kept within the family. It was

not acceptable to unleash them at wider social gatherings! 'Better out than in' became an unofficial family motto and we'd always share a giggle if one of us transgressed at a family meal. Once when we were driving back from Devon my sister and I shared a can of coke and devised a competition to see who could burp the loudest and longest. My sister won hands down!

As the youngest in the family I had a tendency to show off and 'get a bit out of hand' as my mother would say; I tended to test the boundaries more than Rachel, who had a sense of responsibility marginally more developed than mine, probably because she was the eldest. She's four years older, much more practical and extremely kind. She is, quite simply, one of my best friends as well as my sister. I love making her laugh and watching her whole face crease up with delight if I tell her something funny or mimic someone we both know. We've developed an emotional short-hand — if we catch each other's eye in company we often know what the other is thinking. She's almost as great a giggler as I am and we frequently have to walk away from each other in order to maintain a modicum of control and decorum.

When we were little, Rachel wielded all the authority by dint of being the oldest. She founded the Whirligig Club with her friends and I was allowed in on sufferance, but not before I was made to eat a flower from the garden, a rule that did not apply to other would-be members. The flower made me feel slightly sick, but the social cachet of being a member was too great to ignore. We fought verbally but not physically, apart from the occasional wrist-pinching and Chinese burns, expertly administered while Ma wasn't looking. There was a great deal of scowling, sticking out of tongues and name-calling; I was known as Elephant Ankles and she was always Hippo-Bum! Miraculously, although we still jokingly call each other rude names on occasion, we've grown very close and enjoy sharing time together. I remember feeling very protective on holiday, when, aged nine and thirteen respectively, we were clambering over rocks after buying ice-creams. Three boys, led by a tubby dead-ringer for Richmal Crompton's Hubert Lane, chased after her, shouting 'Let's ping her bra strap'. I saw her cheeks burn with embarrassment as we scrambled over the rocks to the safety of the family car. Feeling emboldened by the proximity of the car and our parents, I turned, stuck out my tongue and yelled at them to shove off. They were so surprised, we gained a vital few seconds on them and no bra straps were ever pinged.

There was a short time when we didn't appear to have much in common – I was ten and still hoping to be a cowboy, a footballer or a petrol pump attendant when I grew up, while Rachel had embarked on her teens with her hair in curtains that hid most of her face, a slightly sulky expression and, to the outside world, a withering disregard for her younger sister. Underneath that attitude, however, she was kind and caring; crucially, we never lost the ability to make each other laugh to the point of collapse, and shared humour was the bond between us. I was always proud of her musical achievements; she sang, and played the piano and organ very well, becoming the Organ Scholar at school. She played with great verve and brio and I loved hearing her play the music of Bach, Brahms and Mendelssohn. I used to sit alongside her on the organ bench in our local church, turning the pages while she practised. I don't think she realised at that stage how proud of her I felt.

Nowadays we share a lot of interests and like to do things together, especially walking. Rachel sings in two large London choirs and I try to get to the concerts she is singing in whenever I can. She has always been very supportive of the things I've done in my career, acting as a sounding board when life wasn't running smoothly, but always delighted with my successes. She's the first person I ring when I've got good news to tell. My friends frequently tell me how much they like her and how lucky I am to get on so well with her. They're right — there's absolutely no guarantee that you will grow up to like and be close to your siblings, so I know how fortunate I am. I don't, however, want to portray her as a paragon — we have arguments and she can be bossy, which I suppose is the prerogative of an older sister, but she's a woman of great integrity and loyalty whom I admire and love in equal measure.

When I was growing up my hero was William Brown,

Richmal Crompton's wonderful fictional creation. I read her books voraciously as a child and still enjoy reading them now. I was a classic tomboy and longed to have my own gang of Outlaws. I also wanted my version of Jumble the dog, but my father was allergic to cats and dogs so my sister and I had to be content with Scamp the hamster. I was a rumbustious, spirited child and loved to roam around the local park with my friends Anthony and Robert, skimming stones in the river and generally getting very dirty.

My prized possessions were a pair of red jeans, Harlem Globetrotter black and white baseball boots and a 'Man from Uncle' black briefcase filled with a spy's essential accoutrements – a plastic Luger pistol and a walkie-talkie disguised as a cigarette packet. When I wasn't busy being a spy, I raced around on my bicycle at speed, perfecting a sideways slide to bring it to a halt in the style of speedway riders that I'd watched on television. It seemed awfully boring to slow the bike decorously using the brakes. After a while the bicycle seemed a bit tame, so my father fitted a black device on the frame that mimicked the sound of a motorcycle engine. I was delighted with this added dimension to my bike-riding and remember the joy of listening to the low growl as I cycled through the park. I recall it as a moment of pure happiness – the freedom of independence that the bike gave me, the wind on my face and in my hair, wearing my favourite red jeans and blue windcheater and the little engine 'revving' satisfactorily.

In the 1960s, before the advent of compulsory seat belts, children sat in the back of a car without restraint. When I was very young I often used to stand behind my parents' seats looking straight ahead through the middle of the windscreen. One Sunday afternoon we were driving along a dual carriageway, with a central reservation overgrown with bushes and young trees. Ahead of us a car turned right as if to do a U-turn and get on the dual carriageway heading in the opposite direction. Instead it kept on turning, in effect doing an 'O-turn', ploughed through the central reservation, accelerating all the time, and hit our car amidships. We ended up wrapped round an unforgiving lamp-post, which bent over and badly dented the roof.

Our car was a virtual write-off and I was thrown around in the back like a rag-doll. I was only seven and was badly shocked by what had happened. The noise of tearing metal had been frightening and I was also bleeding heavily from a nasty gash on the top of my head. I stood next to my parents waiting for an ambulance to arrive; we all felt sore and stiff and our spectacular bruises would soon manifest themselves. The police at first couldn't believe what had happened until they saw the tyre marks. A learner driver had been at the wheel and had panicked for some reason; her husband, sitting next to her, did nothing to avert a crash, such as grabbing the wheel or yanking on the hand-brake. To compound an uncomfortable situation, the woman had hysterics at

the sight of my bloodied face and had to be slapped in the
face by the ambulanceman. We were all taken to hospital and checked over; fortunately, none of us had broken
anything and we were soon allowed home.

Over the next few weeks all our aches and pains blossomed, but there were no lasting ill effects. The cut on my
head healed and I was very proud of my multi-coloured
and extensive bruises. The shock of the accident didn't
stay with me and I soon forgot about it. I think it affected
my parents much more, because they saw the car coming
straight at them out of the bushes and knew a collision
was imminent and couldn't be avoided. When the case
came to court Mr and Mrs Bottle entered a not guilty plea,
much to the annoyance of the police. They really were
called Bottle and so the accident was inevitably referred
to as the Bottle–Green case!

Pat and Tony Sherwood and their children, Tim and
Stephanie, were our closest family friends and have
remained so, in spite of the geographical distance between
us. They lived in the Midlands and would visit us in London at Easter-time, or we would travel up to them. We
shared a lot of laughter and fun together and had some
good childhood adventures. There was roughly a two-
year age gap between each of the four children – Tim
was the eldest, then my sister Rachel, Stephanie and me. I
followed Tim around like a devoted acolyte, getting into
scrapes, the muddier and dirtier the better. Rachel and
Stephanie did what I regarded as girly things like ballet.

While Tim and I marauded round the garden, the two girls would be in the garage practising their jetés and pirouettes. One day Tim and I locked them in without their realising and went in pursuit of further adventures; they only discovered they couldn't get out when they were called in for lunch. To my great delight a desperate banging started up from inside the garage. Tim and I kept quiet about what we had done, but we were soon rumbled; the key was handed over reluctantly and the girls emerged relieved, but slightly resentful! Rachel declared she would never play with me again; this upset me, but as we were then given rice pudding for dessert, the feeling was only momentary. And talking of rice pudding – at that age I seemed to specialise in tipping my bowl or plate off the table and onto the floor. This wasn't deliberate, but probably the result of my eagerness to eat what was placed in front of me; I expended a lot of energy as a child and had a healthy appetite. One lunchtime the inevitable happened. I was probably rushing, in order to make more time for adventures; the bowl slipped off the table and fell upside-down – naturally – on the carpet. My mother rolled her eyes and told me off for being careless; Pat was remarkably understanding, while my father and Tony just laughed. I was more concerned that I wasn't going to get any more rice pudding, but was soon mollified when another helping appeared.

I was about six when our two families visited Boscobel House in Shropshire; it's famous for its role in the escape of King Charles II after the Battle of Worcester in 1651. He took refuge at Boscobel and spent the night hiding in a nearby oak tree. The guide who took us round the house looked rather severe and regarded us warily. We were the only people visiting and she seemed to look upon us as a potentially disruptive group, probably with good reason. My father was genuinely interested in the history of the place, but the other adults took it less seriously. When shown the priest-hole, Tony remarked with a straight face that it was a shame that Charles II wouldn't have been able to watch *Juke Box Jury*, because television reception would have been poor in such a confined space. The guide gave him a look of rich disdain.

We then moved on to view the Royal Oak in which Charles II took refuge. It's now believed to be a direct descendant of the original tree, although sometimes it has been presented as the actual tree. We were looking out of an upstairs window and Pat – who is only small – could just see a tiny sapling nearer the house. In jest she said that surely the king couldn't have hidden in such a puny little specimen. The rest of us laughed, but the guide remained po-faced and refused to join in the joke. At that point we decided that it was time for us to go and we trooped out in search of tea, still laughing. The guide couldn't hide her relief when we left! Fifty years on, my parents and Tony no longer alive, the rest of us all still laugh at the memory of Boscobel.

When I was fifteen, I spent a week with Pat at the

primary school where she was deputy head. I wasn't sure at that stage what I wanted to do with my life so decided to shadow her at work. The school was in a deprived area and large numbers of the children came from broken homes and dysfunctional families. When I was first introduced to Pat's class they gathered round me like playful little puppies, all vying for my attention and keen to tell me their latest news. They couldn't pronounce my name so called me 'Scarlitt'. I found them fascinating because they were so full of energy and exuberance. They lived in the moment and seemed to be happy, in spite of any problems at home. I used to read with them and found them responsive and keen to learn; if you praised them, which I did often in order to encourage them, they visibly blossomed and tried harder.

At the annual sports day, they were all beside themselves with excitement, throwing themselves around the field in pure joy. There were cries of 'Scarlitt, look at me' as they lined up for their races; they wanted to be acknowledged and admired, because nobody took much notice at home. I would wave at them and cheer loudly; at the end of the race I was engulfed by hordes of little people, falling over themselves to catch my attention. I often wonder what happened to them in later life and hope that they managed to create happy relationships of their own.

I've always enjoyed reading to children and helping them to enter an imaginative world. They never seem to tire of favourite stories and you have to be prepared to read to them endlessly. *Peter Pan* was a great favourite of the small son of another friend. I threw myself too energetically into the role of Captain Hook, however, and we had to stop because he was getting too frightened. After that we read *Peter Pan* together without any reference to Captain Hook, until he grew old enough to relish Hook's exploits rather than be fearful of them.

I also like the fact that children love to tell jokes and can't stop laughing while they do it. Some of the jokes are terrible and make you groan out loud, but others are genuinely funny. I remember being asked who was the most elastic man in the Bible – the answer came with a triumphant hoot of laughter. Apparently it is Joseph, who tied his ass to a tree and walked to Jerusalem!

We used to listen to the radio a great deal at home and it was always on when I came home from school. I have vague memories of listening to *The Petticoat Line* while I had my tea, as well as *The Archers*. My sister remembers me as a small child standing right in front of the radio, my face about half an inch away from the set, listening intently to the warm, reassuring tones of Daphne Oxenford as she uttered the immortal words 'Are you sitting comfortably? Then I'll begin.' Rachel was convinced that I thought that the voices were coming from tiny creatures inside the radio.

Round the Horne was a great family favourite, as was *The Navy Lark* and *The Men from the Ministry*. Before long I could recall great chunks of the former, without fully comprehending the fabulous double entendres. The voices of Kenneth Williams, Kenneth Horne and Leslie Phillips were as familiar to me as the adult voices of family and friends. That's why it was so delightful to meet and work with Barry Took on *The News Quiz* all those years later, and to be able to tell him in person how funny and inventive his scripts for *Round the Horne* and *Beyond Our Ken* were.

Throughout my childhood my father was always a source of great mischief and impishness. He was an incorrigible tease, and my mother often used to tell him to stop, sensing that her children's patience was being sorely tested. When we were little he would occasionally brush our noses with a wet flannel to wake us up, or resort to tickling our feet and throwing off the bed-sheets. We would groan and sigh, adopting an air of exasperation, but really we enjoyed it.

Pa's pièce de résistance took place during a family holiday in north Cornwall. Harry Roberts, an armed robber who had recently shot dead a policeman in Shepherd's Bush and was on the run, was the subject of much fevered speculation in the media. I had read the story in the newspapers and was worried that he had followed us to Cornwall and was lurking in a cave near the beach. We were walking down the pretty main street in Port Isaac; the rest of the family had gone on ahead and I was ambling along behind them, lost in my own thoughts and probably yearning for an ice-cream. Pa waited for me and we walked together past an old-fashioned bric a brac shop. There was a suit of armour propped up on a pole by the door and we stopped to look at it. With deadly casualness my father said, 'Harry Roberts is hiding inside there.' I shot off down the hill in alarm and didn't stop running until I found my mother and sister. Breathless and anxious I told them that Harry Roberts was coming after us in a suit of armour. My mother's reassurances did nothing to calm my anxiety, nor did the sight of my father laughing as he joined us, amused by his own joke. He spent the rest of the afternoon trying to convince me that Harry Roberts was nowhere near Port Isaac, but I still cowered behind the wind-break, certain that he would rear up from every nook or cranny in the nearby rocks, like Magwitch in *Great Expectations*.

I found beach holidays a mixed blessing. I loved swimming and surfing, as well as building sandcastles and damming little streams that criss-crossed the beach. What I loathed, however, was the hot sun burning my skin and the discomfort of wet sand on my body when struggling to get dry after a swim. I had very blonde hair as a small child and very fair skin; every summer I would suffer on the beach as the sun caused a particularly uncomfortable heat rash, which covered my arms, hands, legs and feet. In the evenings my mother would cover me with calamine lotion to counteract the effect of the sun's rays. It never seemed to work and only added to my discomfort once it had dried and formed cracks on my skin. This then had to be wiped off with a wet flannel, an uncomfortable and even painful task. Fifty years later, I remember the hot, pulsing itchiness of my skin as I lay in bed at night, hoping that sleep would come and put a temporary end to my misery. One day my fingers were accidentally trapped in a car door by a family friend. It was a moot point as to which hurt the most — the throbbing pain in my trapped fingers or the unceasing prickly itchiness of my skin.

My dislike of the feel of wet sand on the soles of my feet and in between my toes manifested itself at a very early age. Warm, soft sand was a positive joy to scrunch my toes up in, but the wet variety was horribly gritty and scratched my skin, particularly when it had somehow insinuated itself into my towel. I must have looked a quaint child, sitting on the beach with a white floppy sun hat on to protect my head, a long-sleeved shirt to keep the sun off my arms and an expression of distaste on my face as I curled my toes in a vain attempt to keep them dry. The enjoyment of swimming and surfing was invariably marred by the knowledge that afterwards I would have to struggle to get dry under a towelling wrap-around, the dreaded sand finding its way everywhere, especially into my pants.

I lost my favourite pair of red T-bar sandals at Trebar-with Strand at the age of four. I mourned their loss for days afterwards and was inconsolable until another pair was purchased. We had all been watching the tide come in from a vantage point on the rocks, marvelling at the speed at which it approached, over-running all the little rock pools and greedily lapping at our toes. As we stepped back a foot or two with each new wave, we realised too late that my shoes had been left on a prominent rock just ahead of us. The sea gobbled them up with relish and they bobbed away, agonisingly just out of reach. My only other childhood mishap at the seaside was when, aged four, I wandered unawares into a kickabout on the beach and got smacked in the face with a hard, wet, gritty football. I don't remember much else about it, apart from the shock of being hit and the fuss everybody made of me afterwards. It certainly didn't put me off the beautiful game! There is one other, somewhat bizarre memory from that holiday – the man who'd inadvertently kicked the football in my face had an arm which had been amputated at the elbow. I had got friendly with his daughter and we regularly took his false arm and hand out of the glove box in his car and ran around with it on the beach. Nobody seemed to notice, oddly, so we had free rein with this intriguing new toy and even used it to dig a sandcastle!

I don't know why I became so obsessed with cigarettes and smoking when I was a small child, but I often used to pick up cigarette butts in the street and start to put them in my mouth, much to the horror of my mother. She strongly discouraged this habit, but my fascination with fags grew stronger. I think I liked the smell of the smoke when the cigarette was freshly lit, and used to watch intently as the smoke was inhaled and then blown out. A friend of my father's could blow smoke rings, a talent that fascinated me even more. One day our next-door neighbour invited us in for tea; I was about five and quite an adventurous child, happy to try new experiences. Wilfred, our neighbour, proffered a beautiful mahogany cigarette box to my parents; they didn't smoke and politely refused the offer. As a joke he offered the box to me – I promptly took a cigarette, put it between my lips and waited for it to be lit. Wilfred was so surprised – and amused – by my response that it took him a while to stop laughing and recover his breath. My parents were laughing too, but gently took the cigarette off me; I couldn't understand why I wasn't being allowed to smoke it. After all, it had been offered to me!

Given my youthful obsession, it's perhaps surprising that I didn't grow up to be a chain-smoker. I had the odd cigarette during my teens, taking surreptitious drags in my bedroom while supposedly doing my homework. Although the window was wide open to disperse the telltale smoke, my mother always knew what I'd been up to. She wasn't heavy-handed in her disapproval, but warned me of the possible health dangers. This was clever as I had a slight tendency to hypochondria in my teens and therefore took note of what she was saying, rather than dismissing it with an irritated shrug. I was also keen

on sport and didn't want to compromise my fitness. A
friend's illness and subsequent death from lung cancer
also had a huge impact on me; it was unbearably dis-
tressing to watch someone I was close to struggle for
breath. A simple conversation would take ages, as every
two or three words were punctuated by another laboured
breath. I decided the supposed allure and glamour of
cigarettes were not worth the huge price paid in loss of
functioning lungs and general good health. Later, when
I became an announcer and newsreader, I had good reason to be grateful for my decision. My voice had become
my livelihood and it was inconceivable that I would ever
knowingly put it at risk.

Tattoos became another obsession of mine when
young and started while reading the comic strip adventures of Popeye, who had an anchor tattooed on his arm.
This intrigued me and I tried to transfer it onto my own
arm with a biro. I then grew more adventurous and drew
all sorts of pictures on my arms, sometimes adding a
touch of red biro to add colour contrast. There was also
a sprinkling of hearts with 'I love Mum' underneath, but
they usually ended up wonky because of the difficulty of
drawing them on my own arm. I decided to experiment
on my friend Robert, using my mother's lipsticks. They
looked quite impressive – bold strokes in red or pink all
down Robert's arms, but they smudged easily and therefore didn't last. The effect on my mother's lipsticks was
catastrophic, much to her annoyance. Robert and I were

delighted when we discovered that we could buy transfers and stick them on our arms. They looked very professional and lasted much longer than our own efforts.

Tattoos have become mainstream and it seems that every other footballer now sports a 'sleeve', where the entire arm is covered in swirling patterns and multi-coloured inks. I think it's sad that beautiful young skin is ruined in this way, and ruined permanently. My childhood obsession has turned into a genuine dislike – I think tattoos look unsightly even on youthful skin, never mind the wizened skin of old age. Some tattooists are, unfortunately, poor spellers; it must be mortifying to carry round with you for the rest of your life a quotation or motto that is spelt wrongly. I am not remotely tempted now to get my skin inked – not even a tiny, discreet butterfly in a place where the sun don't often shine.

One of my happiest memories from childhood was a family holiday to Switzerland. We had a wonderful time walking in the Bernese Oberland, and my sister and I relished all the new experiences – the countryside and mountains, the different food and the strange language. I was seven and looked like Heidi, with very blonde hair and two immaculate plaits, which my mother would tie with red ribbon. Every morning at breakfast an older German couple would come in, smile and pat me on the head. Their eighteen-year-old daughter did the same. I began to enjoy the attention and tried to sit in the same seat each day. My sister, miffed that she wasn't getting the same level of friendly acknowledgment, vied with me to sit in the prime position at the table. There was an unseemly rush for the seat and lots of pushing and shoving – suddenly we didn't seem quite so angelic! In spite of a relative lack of knowledge of each other's language our two families became quite close and kept in touch. We met them again about ten years later at their home in Düsseldorf and spent a very enjoyable day. At one point their daughter, Hannelore, pointed to a beautiful tree in resplendent autumnal colours and exclaimed that it was a gorgeous 'bloody beech'. She meant a copper beech of course, but the saying became part of family lore. As has a remark made by another German friend of mine when we went to an exhibition at the Royal Academy. She looked at a painting by an artist whose name and work I've now forgotten and said, 'I've never been able to come to gropes with his work'!

Our return journey from the holiday in Switzerland was a real adventure for my sister and me, but probably less so for our parents. It started well enough with Rachel and I seated in the back of the family's Ford Anglia playing I-spy and counting the number of cattle that had huge, decorated cow bells hanging round their necks. I was wearing a green felt Tyrolean hat with a feather in it and had a small toy pipe in my mouth, wooden and curly in the traditional style. I'd been asked what I would like to take home as a souvenir and the hat and pipe were what I had chosen! Rachel, more conventionally, chose a music box in the shape of a Swiss chalet. It had a very irritating tune, which got slower and slower as the clockwork mechanism wound down.

Once into France a large stone thrown up by a lorry in front smashed into our windscreen and the glass instantly resembled crazy paving. Unable to see properly, my father guided the car to the side of the road and punched out the glass in front of his seat. We then had to drive through France with an enormous insect collection stuck in a bloodied mess on the back window; we were also frozen and windswept. I remember my father driving as fast as the Ford Anglia would go along straight French roads to get us to the ferry that evening. We didn't quite make it to Calais and had to stay the night in a filthy hotel seemingly in the middle of nowhere. Supper was a very rudimentary affair, enlivened for me by the man at the next table taking out an entire set of false teeth and putting them in a glass of water. That night I read a Professor Branestawm story to my sister, but neither of us could settle down to sleep. We were bitten by various bedbugs throughout the night and Rachel had a nightmare about a French onion seller climbing in through the window; we were all relieved to leave the next morning. Once at Calais the ferry crew took pity on us and we were allowed on first. The rest of the journey was unremarkable, once we'd had the windscreen repaired. When I look back on that holiday now, I remember the warmth of the sun, the gorgeously pure air in the mountains, running through meadows in sheer delight, and lots of laughter and fun with my family. And of course the little curly wooden pipe!

Chapter 3

SCHOOL AND CHILDHOOD ESCAPADES

THE SAD FACT was that the holidays came to an end and school had to be returned to. I went to Haberdashers' Aske's School for Girls, then in Acton, and never really enjoyed it until I got into the sixth form, when we were allowed more autonomy and independence. I was quite naughty and loved to mimic some of the teachers, particularly one of the maths teachers who had a very distinctive way of saying *Quod Erat Demonstrandum*, when she'd solved a knotty mathematical problem. There would be a faint echo from me at the back of the class followed by muffled giggles from my friends. Maths bored me rigid and it was far more interesting to indulge in low-level disruption. The teacher was gentle and kind; when I went back to speak to the school at an Old Girls event many years later, she very generously told me that she always knew that I would end up doing something interesting.

I loved drama and did a lot of plays and readings at school. My childhood was full of books and music, which laid the foundations for a lifelong love of reading and music and a deep appreciation of acting and live theatre. As I grew up, people often remarked on my voice and said I should use it in some way in my future life. This became a leitmotif throughout my time at school and university. My mother had a beautiful speaking voice – very clear and distinct, melodious and possessing great warmth. She was a gentle, loving person and her voice reflected these qualities. I deeply regret that I never recorded her voice while she was alive; it was such an important component of her compassionate self. She read to me a great deal when I was small and this shared experience was one of the delights of my childhood. I used to be entranced by her voice and the unfolding story she was telling. I would inhale her scent – Arpège by Lanvin – and to this day experience a Proustian memory of this scene if I smell the scent at a perfume counter. My mother had very soft skin and as she was reading I'd rub the indentations made by the links of her watch strap on the tender skin around her wrist. As a small child I don't think I was ever happier than at those moments. When she grew old and frail my sister and I would take it in turns to regularly cream and moisturise her skin. She enjoyed this little ritual and it had the practical benefit of stopping her skin becoming too dry and brittle. It was one of the small things we could do to give her pleasure as physical frailty gradually overcame her. It was harrowing to see how rapidly her ability to live a full and active life left her, until she became bedridden in her own home and ultimately in a nursing home, where she needed oxygen and nursing care round the clock. Her mischievous spirit never left her, however, in spite of the many indignities old age conferred on her. The nursing staff loved her, not least for her sense of humour, and would often be round her bed teasing her and making her laugh.

My mother encouraged me to act at school, knowing how much I enjoyed it. I remember aged ten playing a Turk, complete with elaborate headdress, and feeling terribly exotic. This was the occasion when I uttered my first spoonerism. I had to clap my hands in front of a belly-dancing harem played by my classmates – most of whom were trying to make me laugh – and issue an order. Unfortunately, it came out wrong as 'Go and fetch some sharbet and be sherp!' – but it made the audience of parents and siblings roar with laughter. The power of comedy.

My very first appearance on the stage at school occurred when I was seven. Every year the school had a Charity Day, when decisions on how to allocate the regular charity collections in each class were made by the school. Ten girls of varying ages spoke to the school on behalf of a particular charity and the school then voted to decide how much of the total amount each charity should receive. The charity I represented was the Sunshine Home for Blind Babies and I recall asking the girls and staff to close their eyes and try to imagine being blind. I also remember how lonely it felt to be up on stage on my own, looking out at a hall full of upturned faces and trying to project my voice to the four corners of the vast room. The relief when I finished my speech and walked off to applause was immense. I'd been the youngest girl giving a speech that day, but the experience didn't put me off. I went on to play the Queen of Hearts in a dramatisation of *Through the Looking-Glass*, declaiming with great gusto 'Off with their heads' at every possible moment. Other parts followed, notably Badger in a dramatisation of *The Wind in the Willows* and John Proctor in *The Crucible* by Arthur Miller, a play that I came to love and a role that I thoroughly enjoyed playing. It was an all-girls school, so the deep, complex male roles were always an added bonus. I was often picked to recite poetry as well and learned John Betjeman's 'Hunter Trials' off by heart at the age of eight for a concert of music and readings. It still makes me chuckle today.

The school's annual carol service is held at St Martin in the Fields church in Trafalgar Square and I was chosen to read a lesson there as a form representative when I was fifteen. I was delighted to be asked back to read a lesson as a representative of the Old Girls in 2012 and felt quite emotional when the whole school filed in and filled up the pews, the girls all dressed in the familiar green uniform.

Swimming lessons were a highlight of the summer term. The school had an outdoor heated pool and it was fun to leave the classroom and splash around blissfully for half an hour or so. I don't remember the water being particularly warm, and the rudimentary showers NEVER seemed to heat up. We wore hideously unattractive, baggy swimming costumes, which flattered nobody, whatever their size and shape. On our heads we wore either a red swimming cap or a white one. The red cap denoted a beginner, someone who was unable to stray from the shallow end or negotiate a length of the pool. A white cap indicated that the wearer had proved their proficiency by jumping in at the deep end and swimming a length of the pool. When Rachel gained her white cap she proudly wore it in the paddling pool in our garden, which seemed a bit excessive to me!

When I first started swimming lessons, twenty-five red caps would bob about in the shallow end, with much splashing and excited screeching. The less proficient wore red water wings to aid buoyancy and were occasionally hoisted out of the water on the end of a long bamboo pole wielded by our swimming teacher. She was a tall, straight-backed woman who was rumoured to have competed in the Olympics. She had great grace and poise and taught us very well. There was much consternation the day one child's water wing on her left arm burst, instantly making her lopsided and prone to disappearing under the water. The bamboo pole was immediately deployed and she was lifted free from the water and deposited by the side of the pool. We watched fascinated as this spectacle unfolded, and some of us then did our utmost to sabotage the water wings of other children. I also remember that if a child hovered for too long by the steps leading out of the pool, it was a fair bet that they were having a surreptitious pee! If they were discovered in this act of micturition, they were immediately hauled out and sent back to the classroom in disgrace.

During exam time we had 'silent' swimming, since the swimming pool backed onto the gym and sports hall where the exams were held. It was virtually impossible to swim silently, particularly if you were an exuberant seven-year-old for whom part of the joy of swimming was the splish, splash, splosh of the water. As we got older we took part in swimming galas, races and life-saving exams. This entailed swimming a certain number of lengths in pyjamas, taking them off while treading water and then inflating them to use as a Heath Robinson-style buoyancy aid. It was tough to carry off successfully.

Princess Margaret once visited the school and was taken to the pool to watch a swimming display in which I was taking part. She stayed for only about five minutes, during which time she smoked a cigarette in a very stylish, elegant cigarette-holder. Afterwards I was told off for having grass-stained knees, which I had displayed to HRH as I prepared to start a back-crawl race.

Once in our teens, swimming lost a little bit of its appeal and it became a chore to get undressed in a cold cubicle, paddle through a small shallow pool of disinfectant, swim for half an hour and then have to get dry with a rough towel. We hit upon the idea of five-week periods, daring the swimming teacher to call our bluff and make us swim. She usually didn't, deciding that the issue wasn't worth an argument; she did, however, tell us to see a doctor as such lengthy periods were most unusual! She knew exactly what we were up to, but wisely stepped back from a confrontation. Ultimately we were the losers by missing out on what I now regard as an enjoyable activity.

I used to loathe sewing lessons at school and regarded them as a necessary evil to be endured. When I was eight my form teacher, knowing how much I hated needlework, took pity on me and allowed me to read to the form instead. As I looked out at twenty-five heads bent over their sewing I felt immensely grateful to her. The needlework room was a place I ventured into only for the compulsory weekly sewing lesson; I disliked the sewing teacher, who was a stern and strict Scot. One day when I was ten I had attacked the sewing machine treadle with too much vigour and broke the whole thing. I also wrecked the skirt, with its elasticated waist, that I was very reluctantly attempting to make. Miss H. came over, fixed me with her beady, coal-black eyes and informed me that I was 'a very silly little girl'. This was said in a Scottish accent with an attractive rolling of the 'r' sound. After the lesson was over I was soon repeating this phrase to my friends, complete with exaggerated rolling of the 'r' in the words 'very' and 'girl'. Miss H. seemed to regard the fact that I would be the only girl not wearing a skirt of her own creation on the last day of term as punishment enough. I was delighted – I lived in jeans at home and never wore a skirt or dress if I could help it. The thought of parading in a hideous, shapeless skirt filled me with horror, so I was thrilled when I realised I would avoid that particular form of torture. My relationship with Miss H., characterised by extreme wariness on either side, was irrevocably broken when I was caught writing 'HELL' on the label on the door of the needlework room. It did not end well. In all subsequent lessons my feeble attempts at raffia-work, cross-stitching and crochet work were subjected to withering scorn and contempt. This tyranny only ended when Miss H. retired. I have never picked up a needle in earnest since then, apart from sewing on buttons. I can't say my life has been the poorer for it, although I admire the work of those who can sew beautifully.

I committed other minor indiscretions during my time at school, usually as the result of a dare, which I could never seem to resist. I once appeared late for a Latin lesson dressed in tunic, thick-knit red socks and big black lacrosse boots, the studs tapping on the floor as I walked to my desk. A friend of mine, dressed in a similar fashion and complicit in the dare, stood by my side as Miss C., the classics mistress, paused in her lesson and surveyed us both. She very calmly told us that our footwear and socks were completely inappropriate for a Latin lesson and would we please go and change. We complied immediately; as we left the room there was a faint cheer from those who had set the dare.

I often seemed to be wearing the wrong clothing at inappropriate times at school. Another notable 'wardrobe malfunction' occurred when I was about six and fell in the school pond, attempting to jump from one side to the other. It was a small pond and therefore an easy jump to make, but the rock I was perched on gave way at the critical moment of take-off and I fell in up to my waist. The water was dirty and weed-ridden and when the school matron undressed me and gave me dry clothes, we discovered a water-snail in my pants. I was tall for my age and Matron overestimated the clothing size I would need. As a result I was given a huge Aertex shirt and the biggest pair of navy pants the school possessed. They had to be held up with safety pins and flapped around my knees, utterly shapeless. When my mother turned up to collect me and saw me in all my baggy glory, she burst out laughing. For a short while I enjoyed my notoriety as 'the girl who fell in the pond', but life soon returned to normal. It had been worth it. While I was being dressed as Orphan Annie by Matron I managed to miss a Maths lesson!

I sang in the school choir and loved it, although that didn't stop me being naughty during singing lessons. Shakespeare's 'Where the bee sucks, there suck I' from *The Tempest* was sung – inevitably – with the substitution of the word 'suck' by a very similar-sounding Anglo-Saxon expletive. This was regarded as impossibly daring by our thirteen-year-old selves. Our singing teacher would stop playing the piano and enquire, with a pained expression on her face, 'Now who is singing that DISGUSTING word?' My friends and I perfected a look of demure innocence in response to the question and somehow escaped detection. We also used to deliberately scoop while singing, much to the teacher's annoyance, as well as clearing our throats in an ostentatious fashion. We must have been a real pain to teach, but as we got older and matured we all really enjoyed singing and forgot about mucking around. Music was a source of great enjoyment and therefore to be taken seriously.

I now have close links with the school and am very impressed with the relaxed, friendly atmosphere there. The headmistress and the deputy head are both charming and have really welcomed me back into the Habs fold. I was particularly pleased to learn that they are Radio 4 aficionados, with a liking for the *Today* programme and *The News Quiz*. When I was at the school some of the teachers seemed to be remote figures who didn't encourage much friendly interaction. A few seemed impossibly old and because of that there was occasionally a great gulf in understanding between teacher and pupil. We were half-afraid of them, which of course didn't encourage mutual understanding.

Most people can name one teacher from their school who had an important influence on their young lives. Mine was Gloria Williams – Miss Williams at school – who taught me English in an exciting, imaginative way and encouraged me to be bold and believe in myself. In my early teens I drifted a little at school, uncertain as to my future direction and unhappy with the constraints and strictness of school life. I loved English and Drama, but other subjects never set my imagination alight in the same way and I didn't see the point in working hard at them. My father, exasperated at my lack of effort, used to call me a ship without a rudder or, in a brief and hilarious moment of linguistic muddle, a bone for nothing idle. He meant a bone-idle good-for-nothing of course, but the alternative was so entertaining we both burst out laughing, even though I was supposedly being told off! My father and I chuckled about that moment for years afterwards. I was, however, in danger of going off the rails, daydreaming throughout the school day, immersing myself in books but paying no heed to lessons.

Until, that is, the advent of Miss Williams. She was
tall and had long, very blonde hair; she wore black-
framed glasses, which she once admitted to me that she
hid behind. Her lessons were fun and illuminating and
I began to look forward to them. In one lesson she read
aloud from an essay on *Jane Eyre* that she said was excellent and worth reading to the class. Slowly it dawned on
me that it was my essay she was reading out and a feeling
of extraordinary pride grew in me. I was so unused to
being singled out for praise that it was a moment of pure
pleasure. From that moment on I stopped daydreaming
and concentrated, keen for her to continue to think highly
of me. Like Dr Stone at university a few years later, she
was constructive in her criticisms and always stressed the
positive. She had a very good sense of humour and made
me laugh; for that reason alone she could do no wrong.
She once took some of my poems to show to the headmistress and they were published in the school magazine.
She was the best sort of teacher – endlessly encouraging,
a good listener who took my sometimes half-baked the-
ories and ideas seriously and argued them out with me.

Miss Williams subsequently became a headmistress
herself and invited me one year to give out the prizes
at her school. Knowing me well, she advised me not to
get the giggles when the vicar read prayers before the
start of the prize giving. She warned me that he had a
very distinctive delivery and that a good proportion of
the girls would start sniggering. All this was said with

a characteristic twinkle in her eye. Forewarned is fore-armed: the rotund vicar – the Word made Flesh – spoke in an extraordinary way, a mixture of Alan Bennett and Mr Bean interlaced with bizarre scoops and a strange whinnying sound. The girls soon started to laugh and weren't very successful in hiding their mirth; I caught Miss Williams's eye and noticed her amused expression. She treated most situations with relaxed amusement, which is why I think she was so popular with all she taught. I don't remember her getting riled or stroppy and she seemed to exude a calm serenity in her lessons, the perfect antidote to teenage girls febrile with rampant hormones and premenstrual tension.

We keep in touch and I look forward to her wry, perceptive comments in her annual Christmas cards. Last Christmas she wrote: 'Make sure you whoop it up a bit – spend rather than save!' I owe a great deal to her and am delighted that she has seen me evolve from a slightly disaffected teenager, determined not to play by the school's rules, to the point I've reached today – still a non-conformist, but focused on what I want to achieve, fulfilled and content.

• • •

MY PARENTS AND sister had all passed their driving tests at the first attempt, so the pressure was on to do the same when I started to have driving lessons. My mother was heavily pregnant with Rachel at the time she took her test, and was convinced that the driving examiner couldn't wait to get out of the car, so wary was he of possibly having to help her give birth!

My instructor was a kind, avuncular man called Mr Casson, who used to entertain me with tales of his other clients, some of whom were known to me. Once when we were heading up the A40 and I was concentrating hard, he made me laugh out loud by describing a woman with billiard-table-shaped legs, who had no feel for the pedals and consequently braked and accelerated hard, lurching him back and forth in his seat. Another story involved a rather pompous teenage boy who dressed in a cravat and tweed jacket, and who objected to wearing a seat belt because it would crease his clothing. He was full of apocryphal stories and reckoned he'd once seen a Reliant Robin do a wheelie on the motorway! Mr Casson was known not only for his success in getting his pupils to pass their driving test, but also for his quaint phrases. He often used to say 'Now, just a little more noise than a lady likes to hear' when I was attempting a hill start and trying not to rev the engine.

On the day of my test I was, understandably, a bit anxious. Mr Casson drove me to the test centre, as was his custom on the day of the test, and tried to relax me by drawing on his fund of funny stories. He likened me to his pet poodle – alert, but over-anxious! The test went well until we got to the moment of the emergency stop. I was told to carry out this procedure once the test examiner tapped his clipboard on the dashboard. For some reason he never did this, so I spent the rest of the test in a state of hyper-anticipation, foot hovering over the brake pedal, waiting for the tap that never came. Fortunately, at the end of the test, the examiner told me that I'd driven well and that he was passing me. I went back into the test centre grinning inanely. Mr Casson was delighted and said he'd drive me back home, for tradition's sake. When my mother saw him pull up outside the house she immediately thought I'd failed and couldn't understand why I was smiling so much. I soon put her right and we celebrated accordingly – I was thrilled that I'd maintained the family tradition of passing first time.

. . .

AT THE END of March 2014 my sister and I were invited to the Haberdashers' Aske's Schools Gala Concert, which was held at the Barbican Hall in the City of London. At supper with the headmistress before the concert we discussed our experience of music-making at school; my sister had been one of the Organ Scholars and happily recalled memories of the director of music who had taught her for a time. I decided it was best to keep quiet about my deliberately unorthodox singing in the music room with my friends! The concert itself was terrific and hugely enjoyable, with a high standard of musicianship on display. The Combined Symphony Orchestra comprised both boys and girls; the two schools stand on magnificent, adjacent sites in Elstree. The combined Boys' Prep and Girls' Junior School choirs were delightful and sang very well. Some of them were incorrigible fidgeters while others stood almost to attention. One little girl with big bunches was having a wonderful time, fizzing and crackling with delight. At the end she skipped off stage, completely unfazed by her surroundings and the large number of people in the audience. By contrast, a boy on the end of the front row seemed overawed by the occasion and stood mute, seemingly transfixed by the lighting in the auditorium.

The highlight of the Barbican concert for me was the Boys' School Big Band; I have a penchant for loud brass and they made a great sound. They not only sounded good but they looked good too and had all the moves. One boy in particular caught my eye. He was quite stocky and half the height of the others. As 'Cruisin' for a Bluesin'' took wing he threw his head back and tooted his trumpet with great elan.

I took part in a music concert in the school hall when I was about ten. It was a large and impressive room decorated with replica friezes from the Elgin Marbles and with a pipe organ high up in one corner. I was to accompany on the piano a classmate who was to play the clarinet. I hadn't really practised the piece enough – too busy being a rumbustious football player in the park – which led to an attack of nerves just before going on. This had two consequences – I perched perilously on the very edge of the music stool all the way through the performance, to the point that I nearly fell off; and I also set off at a manically fast pace, like a horse that has bolted. The poor girl playing the clarinet nearly passed out with the effort of keeping up with me. It wasn't my finest hour, but as all my energies were concentrated on being the first female footballer to play for Spurs, it didn't really matter.

All-girls schools sometimes tend towards the feverish and intense, particularly at exam time. If a man ever strayed into the school a collective madness would descend on the girls. One term a male teacher stood in as a temporary replacement for our German teacher and it was as if we had all returned to the eighteenth century, prone to attacks of the vapours. I remember hanging out of a window overlooking the swimming pool with a couple of friends, overexcited and skittish at the sight of this exotic male creature chatting animatedly with the PE teacher. One of our number rashly wolf-whistled, alerting both of them to our position. A look of undisguised distaste flitted over the PE teacher's face as we ducked down from the window and scrambled to get away, half-embarrassed and yet half-exultant.

The subject of sex only featured at school in the form of a biology lesson, which stuck strictly to the physiological facts, with no mention of love and emotions or the complexity of relationships. Spermatozoa, ova and the lining of the womb made for a fairly boring lesson, and I ended up – as I usually did if something bored me – looking out of the window and daydreaming. There weren't even any graphic depictions of male and female genitalia to enliven the occasion. The lesson must have been excruciating for the biology mistress to teach – a class full of sniggering schoolgirls whose tittering reached a crescendo whenever the word 'penis' was mentioned.

Our discussions about sex usually took place on the sports field; in breaks between games of tennis we'd hide underneath the prolific summer canopy of a large willow tree and talk with great authority on the subject. In truth we knew very little about it, but were desperate to appear worldly and sophisticated. Crushes on teachers were common and we debated the relative merits of our favourite staff with great energy. I once fainted on the lacrosse pitch, the result of forgoing a particularly unappetising school lunch. To my great delight I came round in the arms of the PE teacher at the side of the pitch. I'm ashamed to say that I exaggerated how I was feeling in order to enjoy her attentive concern for a few minutes more.

I enjoyed my sports lessons in spite of the fact that my enthusiasm far outweighed my ability. I was a fast runner and liked to run up and down on the wing in lacrosse. It can be quite a brutal game and we were frequently getting cuts and bruises as the result of a tackle. One of my classmates hated the game so much that she used to run in the opposite direction if the ball ever came anywhere near her, much to the frustration of the PE teacher. Sometimes we used to pretend to throw the ball to her, just for the enjoyment of seeing her hare away to the far corner of the pitch. In the depths of winter we wore red knitted sweaters, grey divided skirts, red socks and black lacrosse boots; not for us the luxury of a tracksuit and warm legs. We always seemed to be frozen in spite of endless running around and would often walk into the pavilion with a bad case of chapped skin around the upper thighs.

The summer months on the sports field were much more fun, simply because it was warmer and there were more opportunities to hide away beneath the willow tree. I enjoyed playing tennis but never really took it seriously; it was much more fun to steal away, lie in the sun and laze through the entire afternoon with my friends, talking and laughing. My best friend and I once entered the school tennis doubles competition for a joke and found ourselves in a first round draw against the school champions. If I explain that my friend served all the balls of her opening service game straight into my back, you'll get some idea of the standard we were operating at! We emerged from the match with a little bit of dignity intact, having somehow managed to win a game in each set. One afternoon up at the field my period started; pleading stomach cramps I was allowed to sit and watch Wimbledon in the pavilion on television. It was a titanic struggle between Chrissie Evert and Martina Navratilova and I loved every twist and turn as first one player gained the ascendancy and then the other. It was exhausting to watch and at one point I was told off by the tennis coach for being too vocal in my support! Lured in by my shouts of appreciation, I was gradually joined by other girls and eventually the coach; we watched the match to its exciting conclusion, with Navratilova emerging the winner.

My finest sporting moment was being selected to be a ball girl at the Queen's Club tournament – in those days a mixed event. We were like young colts, excited and a little bit overwrought. This was the early 1970s and sadly we encountered our own version of a creepy middle-aged male who felt he was entitled to a certain 'reward'. One of our group was exceptionally well endowed in the chest department and had an enviable embonpoint, which her white Aertex shirt served only to emphasise. Having once noticed her, this man – an official at the club – began to turn up at every match she was involved in. He did his best to touch her or press himself against her, which made her acutely uncomfortable. Outraged by his presumption and blatant invasion of her personal space, the rest of us loyally formed a phalanx around her wherever she went and managed to keep her unpleasant pursuer at bay. After a couple of days he fortunately lost interest and our friend was able to enjoy the tournament. Innocent as we were, we intuitively knew that this behaviour was wrong. We hadn't expected lechery amidst the lawns and lemon barley water.

As we are now discovering, the early '70s appear to have been a haven for those inclined to foist themselves on young girls and boys. The tennis official we encountered made the casual assumption that he could impose himself sexually on our friend, in spite of her obvious unwillingness to have anything to do with him. It was the twentieth-century version of *droit du seigneur*; he certainly seemed unused to meeting resistance.

Historical sex abuse has made the headlines a great deal over the past two years. In July 2014 Rolf Harris was jailed for five years and nine months for a string of sexual offences on young girls. He had shown no remorse for his crimes and took full advantage of his celebrity status to carry them out. As a child I used to enjoy his shows where he sang songs and painted pictures, all carried out with his trademark bonhomie and good humour. Now I feel disillusioned and sad that he could abuse children's trust so comprehensively.

I fortunately never came into contact with Jimmy Savile at the BBC, but would sometimes see him across the room in the canteen and made sure I kept well away from him. We all commented on how creepy and weird he was. He seemed sinister and unfathomable, which the large cigars, lurid shell suits and extraordinary hair served only to underline. We now know he was committing sexual offences on a horrific scale and with impunity. He fooled so many people and large institutions, such as the BBC, the NHS and the government. Savile never faced trial and was therefore never brought to justice; he was Britain's most prolific sex offender and yet was untouchable because he was a national celebrity. He too exercised the power that came with being famous to commit terrible crimes and cover them up. It is desperately sad for the many people he abused that somehow, incomprehensibly, he was able to escape justice and in the process made us all look stupid.

Happily at Queen's the tennis matches were fun and memorable. I was one of the ball girls for a doubles match in which Billie Jean King and Rosie Casals – then the number one pairing – were playing. Thankfully, none of us sent the balls down the side of the court at the wrong time and didn't get them mixed up when new balls were needed. Afterwards the American pair kindly posed for photographs with us and we cantered off, heady with the excitement of it all. The other match that stood out was between Billie Jean King and Virginia Wade, played on an indoor court because of heavy rain. It was closely fought with great skill shown on either side. Billie Jean eventually won in three sets, much to my disappointment, as Virginia Wade was my sporting heroine at the time. Afterwards our PE teacher told me off for grinning too much whenever Virginia Wade won a crucial point! I still remember large chunks of the match, the delighted roar of the crowd and the echo generated by an indoor court. I became the proud owner of a number of autographs from the crème de la crème of tennis talent at that time. Everyone seemed more relaxed and laid-back then; the game wasn't played with quite such intensity and the players were prepared to talk to their fans, rather than closeting themselves away behind a wall of PR people and agents.

Given that I'd been such a maverick at school, I'm now really enjoying giving something back in whatever way I can. I was delighted and honoured to have a school prize named after me. I think my parents would have been equally delighted to know that their naughty child, who preferred learning the names of the entire first team squad at Spurs to conjugating Latin verbs, was now being invited back to school to hand out prizes. I realise now, although I didn't particularly at the time, that I got a first-class education there as well as useful lessons in the value of open-mindedness, tolerance and compassion. I'm very far from being perfect, but I do try to put those lessons into practice.

Chapter 4

MA AND PA

I'D BEEN GIVEN a Roman centurion's uniform for my sixth birthday; it was what I'd asked for and it turned up in a large parcel wrapped in brightly coloured paper. The uniform consisted of a grey plastic breastplate, grey helmet with a jaunty red feather and a slightly incongruous red and yellow plastic sword. I'd been so thrilled with this gift that I wore it all the time, apart from when I went to school. Early one Saturday morning, when my father was in the kitchen making a cup of tea, I marched in proudly dressed in my uniform. Unfortunately, I tripped over my sword just as I made my entrance, which necessitated a body-swerve that Gareth Edwards would have been proud of and a head-long plunge towards the kitchen sink as I lost my balance. My father, eyes wide at my less than dignified entrance, let out a great guffaw of laughter and just couldn't stop, eventually collapsing onto his knees on the floor. The laughter came in great gusts and his eyes were filled with tears of merriment. Eventually he got up off the floor, gave me a big hug and a kiss and went back to making the tea, still chuckling to himself.

I climbed the stairs to my bedroom feeling elated; I loved making him laugh and was secretly proud that I could do so quite easily. My father had a great capacity for laughter and mischief, as did my mother, but their laughter was benign and completely bereft of cruelty or malice. I think my father – or Pa as I called him – was intrigued by his younger daughter's evident delight in being a tomboy. My role model was the fictional creation William Brown, but I also immersed myself in cowboy literature and asked for a Zane Grey annual every Christmas. I used to play in the garden dressed in a sky-blue cowboy hat, a light-brown fringed bolero, a striped, buckled snake-belt in my jeans and – my pride and joy – a toy gun with caps. If my father was gardening he'd take part in imaginary shoot-outs with me, hiding behind bushes and running between one hiding place and another. His laughter always gave his position away and I was allowed to 'win' the gun battle. He would then put me in the wheelbarrow and trundle me round to the back door in time for tea.

On light summer evenings I used to sit on the window-sill in my bedroom and watch him water the garden. I was supposed to be in bed asleep, but it was much more fun watching him. He never gave any indication of having seen me at the window, but would suddenly fire the hose at me, drenching the window-pane. The first time it happened I was so surprised I fell off the sill onto my bed. I bobbed back up again to see him standing there roaring with laughter; he blew me a kiss and went back to his watering. On subsequent occasions it became a game between us, with me trying to anticipate the moment he would wheel round and aim the hose at the window. Often he would pretend to do it and catch me out as I leapt off the sill prematurely. He never once rebuked me for being out of bed when I should have been asleep.

He was tall and good-looking with naturally wavy hair and kind blue eyes. My sister and I idolised him when we were growing up, because he was funny, fun to be with and kind-hearted. My mother and father were a striking couple in their prime and my sister and I used to be very proud of them when they came to school events. They always looked younger than their years and obviously enjoyed life and being with each other. I remember Pa furling his umbrella tightly, polishing his shoes until they gleamed and brushing his hair with special brushes that lay on the dressing table, before setting out for work. If we were walking with him to the station, my sister and I would have to break into a little trot to keep up with him. He was strong and often took us for rides on his back when we were at the beach, lurching from side to side and suddenly dipping in an effort to get us to fall off. There is an old cine-film of us clinging on desperately until the inevitable happened and we both slowly slid onto the sand. Pa's face was wreathed in smiles and he looks triumphantly into the camera as Grandpa kept filming. We got straight back onto his back and Pa began immediately to bob and dip, seemingly never tiring of our cries of 'Again, again!' and showing endless patience. Another game he enjoyed playing was dubbed 'push the thumb'. He would grasp our hands tightly and then Rachel and I would try our hardest to prise his thumb away, but never succeeded in moving it. He would laugh and tickle us and then pretend that he couldn't push our little thumbs back either.

We used to look forward to staying with Granny and Grandpa because it meant adventures on the beach and rides on the donkeys. Granny, however, was quite strict. My mother sometimes had to strike a somewhat precarious balance between allowing us to be exuberant and boisterous, but reining us in when we were indoors with Granny and Grandpa. Her relationship with Granny, her mother-in-law, was occasionally fraught, particularly if I had been especially high-spirited and lively. One morning, egged on by my sister, I filled my mouth with milk, puffed out my cheeks and popped them. The milk shot out all over the table much to the delight of my sister, the horror of my mother and the consternation of my grandmother. My father struggled not to laugh, while Grandpa's shoulders heaved up and down. He was a more relaxed character than Granny, happy for Rachel and I to run around noisily. The milk incident became part of family lore, along with my penchant for writing my signature and the date on the wallpaper under the light switches.

As a child I was a fast runner and was thrilled to come first in the school flat race and have a red ribbon pinned to my chest, with my parents looking on. The next race was called Horse and Rider, in which a skipping rope was put round the shoulders of the first runner for the second runner to hold onto, as if holding the reins of a horse. As the faster runner I was in front, with my partner, Susan, holding onto the rope. My desire to win overcame any concerns for my partner; I wanted to win again and have another red ribbon adorning my T-shirt. Not far from the finish line and in first position, Susan fell over. Undaunted I kept on running; Susan was still holding onto the rope and I dragged her over the line to finish second. In spite of a few bruises and grass stains on her pristine white T-shirt, she was delighted that she'd won a ribbon, albeit yellow rather than red. I ran over to my parents, but my delight at coming second was soon tempered by their reaction. They felt I should have stopped and helped her up, rather than hauling her to the finish. When I pointed out plaintively that we wouldn't have been second if I'd done that, they gently told me that winning wasn't everything.

My father was Head Boy at Bristol Grammar School and won an exhibition to read classics at Worcester College, Oxford. His studies were interrupted by the Second World War and after two years at Oxford he joined the Ayrshire Yeomanry. He fought in North Africa and Italy, ending up in Carinthia in Austria; the experience inevitably turned him from a boy into a man. He never spoke much about his time as a soldier when we were young, but discussed it with us a little once we'd gone to university ourselves. He fought in an artillery regiment, the huge guns pounding enemy positions. I remember him praising the bravery of his batman, who had volunteered to pick up the body parts of comrades who had been killed when a gun backfired. He also talked about a friend who had been sent on a recce and had been hit by a sniper's bullet; he recalled his body being brought back into camp, unscathed except for a small bullet hole right in the middle of his forehead. In his seventies my father returned to Tunisia to see the battlefields again, to visit the war graves of fallen comrades and to remember those who, as he put it, had been denied fifty extra years of life. He was acutely aware of the randomness of death in the midst of war and never took life for granted. He and my mother often told my sister and me to make the most of every single day and not worry too much about the future, particularly when we were stressed about exams.

They never pressured us or made us feel that we had to achieve and be successful, no matter what. They wanted us to realise our potential and make the most of our talents, but not at the price of unhappiness or the loss of peace of mind.

Pa used to say that the only present he got for his birthday while serving in Africa was a tangerine, and that he spent the day digging trenches. He knew that this always evoked groans and much eye-rolling from Rachel and me and often said it just to get a reaction, laughing all the while. Fortunately, he survived the war without suffering any injury, ending up as a Captain. When he returned to Oxford he switched from classics to politics, philosophy and economics (PPE), and threw himself into student life, albeit as a mature man rather than a callow youth. He took the Civil Service exams, did very well and joined the Air Ministry on graduating. He had a very successful career as a senior civil servant, or, as he styled himself, a 'Whitehall warrior'. He was heavily involved in defence procurement and travelled extensively in Europe and the USA. He found his work intellectually stimulating and loved it; as he grew more senior we would only see him for what is now called 'quality time' at the weekends. Despite that he was a big and important presence in our lives, and Rachel and I loved our conversations and shared laughter with both our parents round the dining table as we grew up.

My father had been deaf in one ear ever since the war

and had attributed this to his proximity to heavy artillery while fighting in North Africa. Thirty years later, when he was in his fifties, it was discovered that he had a benign brain tumour (an acoustic neuroma) growing on the auditory nerve and it was this that had caused his loss of hearing. It was the size of a tennis ball and when discovered was causing him serious problems with his balance and peripheral vision. He went into the London Hospital in the summer of 1978 for an eight-hour operation to remove the tumour. I had just graduated from university and was able to be with my mother throughout his time in hospital and his recovery, before joining the BBC in October. We visited every day and were very fortunate that the MoD agreed that his driver could take us to and from the hospital. On occasion they would send a uniformed military driver who, much to our surprise, would salute as we got in the car. A good friend who lived opposite joked to his young son that we were spies!

My father was a good-looking man and on the day before his operation he looked remarkably well, as if nothing was wrong. Ma and I hugged and kissed him and wished him all the best. Rachel was in Kenya on holiday and had phoned to pass on her love. We were reluctant to leave him that evening and kept looking back as we left the ward. He smiled and waved and looked extraordinarily resilient. The next day Ma and I gardened furiously in order to distract ourselves. Every time the phone rang we jumped and wondered what we were going to hear.

Friends dropped by to comfort and support us, for which we were very grateful. By five in the evening Pa had been in theatre for nearly nine hours. I remember the heat of the sun on my back as I bent over the flower-beds, trying to imagine what was happening to Pa and fervently hoping that the news would be good. Ma and I talked desultorily, half-listening to each other and half-listening out for the phone. When it eventually rang we were told that Pa had come through the surgery well, but that they had had to sever his facial nerve in order to cut out the entire tumour.

When we saw him in intensive care two days later, he was virtually unrecognisable. A huge bandage like a white turban was wound round his head, there was a drain in his head and he looked as if he had had a bad stroke, owing to the cutting of the facial nerve. If I sat on one side of him he was still Pa, good-looking and with mobile features, but on the other side his face drooped alarmingly and the paralysis gave a severe rigidity to his profile. Watching him trying to drink a cup of tea with no control over one half of his mouth was heart-breaking. He'd always been strong, physically and mentally, and here he was struggling to manage simple tasks and talk clearly. It was the very first intimation of his mortality for me and it was a sobering experience.

A subsequent operation grafted a nerve from his tongue onto the severed facial nerve and over a period of some months it gradually lifted his face. He no longer looked like a stroke victim, but he never regained the boyish good looks that he'd had before the surgery. He was still my father, however, with the same ready laugh and quick wit. His speech became much clearer over the following months and he was soon able to hold his own in the family's banter and repartee. We were all thrilled that he'd made such a good recovery and were delighted for him when he returned to work four months later. He wasn't quite the Action Man he'd been before the advent of the tumour, but he had plenty of happy memories such as being winched down from a helicopter onto a recently surfaced submarine, in order to sample life below the waves for a few hours. We teased him mercilessly about this experience, because he'd been winched down with a briefcase in one hand and a rolled-up copy of *The Times* under his other arm. Mercifully, he wasn't wearing a bowler hat, but if he had been he would have looked just like Terry Thomas!

Pa had a long and happy retirement and he and my mother travelled widely in Europe and North America, walking in the mountains that they both loved so much. They would return fit, tanned and very happy, bubbling over with tales of their walks and the beautiful landscapes they had encountered. When they grew old and frail their lives inexorably shrank, their options and choices restricted by infirmity and lack of mobility. It gives me comfort to remember them in their prime when they took such delight in being fit and active.

My father died in May 2007 in his eighty-seventh year. He had become increasingly frail over the preceding three years with respiratory and mobility problems as well as prostate cancer. My mother – who had trained as a nurse – performed minor miracles in caring for him devotedly, and probably compromised her own health in doing so. They had an extraordinarily happy marriage and she demonstrated her love for him in the way she looked after him. Although physically frail, my father's mind remained razor sharp and I cherish the many talks and laughs we had at this time.

When it became clear that my father would not get better and return home from hospital he was moved to a room on his own to the side of the main ward. This gave us complete privacy and we spent Pa's last few days by his bedside, holding his hand, hugging him and telling him how much we loved him. It rained incessantly outside, the weather matching our mood. It's hard watching someone you love dying; it's an inexorable process that you want to stop in its tracks, but are utterly powerless to do so. I watched him closely, hoping that he would open his eyes one last time, but I think he was already on his journey from life to death, a transition that is both profound and unfathomable. He appeared peaceful in spite of his breathing growing stertorous and laboured.

As the machines registered the constant fall in his blood pressure the Sister in charge suggested we go home to get some sleep. We were reluctant to go but were all exhausted and so decided to leave, hoping that he would last through the night. We had barely got into bed when the phone rang and we were summoned back. We walked through the virtually silent hospital and into the ward, unwilling to reach our destination and uncertain as to what lay ahead. We were met by a kind-hearted nurse, who told us that Pa had died just a few moments before we'd arrived. I felt as if I'd received a hard blow to the stomach and realised that life had changed irrevocably. We went into the room and kissed his still-warm face and stroked his hair; his essential spark had departed and his body was an empty husk. I hadn't seen a dead body before, but I knew immediately that there was an absence, a complete lack of the person I had loved so much. Our family now comprised three people, not four, and we hugged each other and cried as we said our goodbyes to a man who had been such an influential and integral part of our lives. I felt as if the guy-ropes that had kept me emotionally grounded and secure had all been ripped out of the earth, leaving me rootless. Seven years on I think about him a lot and am able to remember fondly his laughter, kindness and wisdom. The acute pain and grief of the early days has metamorphosed into a sadness that he is no longer around, but also an ability to laugh at the many happy memories I have of him.

My mother, Ruth, was tall and slender with strikingly auburn hair, hazel eyes and freckles. She was the kindest, gentlest person I have ever met, with a seemingly endless supply of compassion and empathy for everyone, not just her family. My sister and I could not have been luckier to have had such a mother, although we often took her for granted when we were growing up, a fact that pains me a lot now that she is no longer around. She often used to joke and say that we would miss her when she had gone, to which we would invariably roll our eyes and groan. Now, of course, I know that she was absolutely right.

Ma had a tough time growing up because she lost her beloved parents within eighteen months of each other, her father when she was fourteen and her mother when she was sixteen. Both died of conditions that would be easily treatable today – her father in the aftermath of an appendix operation and her mother as a result of an over-active thyroid. Ma was farmed out to a relative who didn't really want to take her in and a time of real unhappiness followed. Her two older brothers were old enough to fend for themselves, but her younger brother was similarly miserable and ran away from the stern, inflexible uncle he'd been sent to live with. Ruth and John were very close in age, with just fifteen months between them, and climbed trees and roamed freely in the fields around their home and generally had an idyllic early childhood. Photographs of them show two contented, happy children. The idyll came to an end a few years later, but despite the immense blow of losing their parents and having to live with unwelcoming, largely indifferent relatives, they both grew up to be kind and loving and possessed of a great sense of humour. They were quick to laugh and loathed pretension and pomposity.

My mother had a strong mischievous streak and was quite naughty at school. She once managed to crawl out of a class unnoticed with a friend; there is a photo of her taken at about the time this happened in which she's proudly wearing clothes from the dressing-up box and looking rebellious. She remained mischievous throughout her life and had many larky tales to tell about her time at the Queen Elizabeth Hospital in Birmingham, where she trained as a nurse. Medical students would wave amputated legs out of windows at her as she passed by, while large bloomers were regularly run up the hospital's flagpole, waving insouciantly in the breeze until noticed by Matron and swiftly taken down. Ma loved to tell the story of the time when, standing at the top of a large grand staircase in the nurses' home with some friends watching guests assemble for a black-tie event many feet below, they leant over in the darkness and shook talcum powder over the gathering, covering everyone with a fine white dust. Hiding in the gloom and peeking over the mahogany banister, their reward was to view many outraged and perplexed faces turning upwards to see who or what had perpetrated this inexplicable act. Ruth often couldn't get through this story without succumbing to laughter. Again it was the pricking of pomposity and pretension that appealed to her.

After her death Rachel and I found a letter that she'd

kept for over sixty years. It was from a soldier who had been sent back to England to recover from injuries suffered while serving abroad during the Second World War. Ruth's maiden name was Mercy and she was therefore known as Nurse Mercy; this soldier wrote praising her nursing skills and caring nature, and noted how appropriate her name was for someone who had chosen to be a nurse. The surname caused much merriment for an elder brother, Edward, who became a professor of geology. Earlier in his career he had gained a PhD and so called himself Dr Mercy – this became funny when he added his initials. He was named Edward Leon Philip and so signed his name as Dr E. L. P. Mercy.

My mother spoke movingly about her experiences nursing during the war, looking after young men who had suffered grievous injuries in battle. She often remembered a boy of eighteen who'd stepped on a mine and lost both his feet; she spoke admiringly of his resilience and refusal to be dragged down by his misfortune. There was a lot of laughter and camaraderie on the wards and my mother's face would light up when she remembered the soldiers and their positive spirit. One day a radio was on in the ward and announced that one of the soldiers lying there had been awarded the Victoria Cross for Gallantry. A great shout went up from the other soldiers, those who could walk went over to his bedside and congratulated him, and Matron came in to shake his hand and proffer a bottle of wine. What my mother remembered in particular was the 'still, small voice' at the centre of this excited hullabaloo. The newly honoured soldier was quiet, shy and modest, completely overcome by being the centre of attention. My mother was attracted to people like that, as am I; we both had a natural aversion to brashness and loud, bumptious personalities.

Other memories my mother spoke about concerned the dull, monotonous but intrusive sound of German bomber planes flying over the Queen Elizabeth Hospital on their way to drop bombs on Coventry. They used the hospital buildings, which were on high ground, as a navigational marker and so would drone overhead night after night. Occasionally, injured German and Italian prisoners of war were brought to the hospital for specialist treatment and the nursing staff were given the option of refusing to nurse them. Some did refuse, but my mother viewed them primarily as injured men who needed help to recover. One Sister, who was an outstandingly good nurse and teacher, tragically learned of her fiancé's death while she was on duty. He was the second fiancé she had lost because of the war; the sombre mood deepened considerably when she was later found dead in her room, having taken a fatal overdose. Both my parents witnessed extremes of human behaviour during the war, as well as physical hardship and austerity. They were very young in age, yet mature. I often wonder if this maturity contributed to such a happy, stable relationship, quite apart from their obvious deep love for each other.

They met when my mother fell off a wall and landed on my father. They were with a nursing friend, Migs, in Birmingham watching the Lord Mayor's Show. They had decided to climb a wall to get a better view; Migs had gone first and was hauling my mother up with my father assisting from below. My mother, however, lost her footing and fell in an awkward heap on my father; she was mortified, whereas my father laughed and found it very amusing. And so began an incredibly happy, deeply loving partnership that lasted until my father's death.

I always marvelled at their marriage because it was a genuine meeting of hearts and minds; they never stopped talking to each other and made each other laugh constantly. There were disagreements and arguments inevitably, but they were resolved swiftly and usually with laughter. There was never any festering resentment or sulking, and disputes were discussed openly and frankly. There was a zero-tolerance policy on sulking in our family and my sister and I were told that it was childish and selfish. We learned early in life that talking openly and honestly was a far better way of solving problems.

From childhood into adulthood my mother and I were always able to talk freely and openly with one another about any subject, whether contentious or anodyne. For a woman of her generation she had surprisingly enlightened and trenchant views on abortion, believing with absolute conviction that it was a woman's right to choose what happened to her body. She used to get quite exercised on the subject, remarking that it was typical of some men to attempt to control every aspect of women's lives. She was a great support during my adolescent years and the tentative steps I was taking to be my own person.

One day while I was home from university, my mother and I were so deep in conversation that we failed to notice that we were trying to walk up a down escalator in a big department store. We managed four steps before falling down flat, one on top of the other. Typically, we couldn't stop laughing and had to make a swift exit to the safety of the restaurant, aware of people's incredulous stares and feeling faintly embarrassed. Over a very welcome cup of tea – something we always loved to share together – we giggled like two naughty schoolgirls. As with my father, I loved being able to make her laugh and can hear her now saying 'Oh Charlie, you are a hoot' – one of her favourite expressions.

As well as being easy to talk to and laugh with, my mother was an excellent listener and was genuinely interested in other people. She would find herself in situations where strangers would confide in her and unburden themselves; they would tell her that they knew she would be sympathetic because she had a kind face. She was a remarkably calm, peaceful person who achieved an extraordinary serenity in her later years, even in the face of great disability when she lost the use of her legs. Lying in bed in the nursing home, propped up on pillows and permanently attached to an oxygen cylinder because of a failing heart and lungs, she poignantly told me that in her dreams she could walk again. She accepted her increasing physical frailty stoically and calmly; I was enormously proud of the way she lived her life during her last few months. With death beckoning she was tranquil and accepting. It was humbling to witness and I hope that when my life is drawing to a close I can accept it with equal stoicism and equanimity.

My mother stood up strongly for what she believed in, particularly if she perceived injustice and unfairness. She fought my corner when, as a twelve-year-old, I had a torrid time at school with my form teacher. This woman was eccentric, but not in a genial way, cantankerous and with a tendency to minor sadism. She probably wouldn't be allowed anywhere near a school now, but in the late '60s she had her own class. The year before I'd been a happy, exuberant child who was form captain and loved drama. I was outgoing and confident, but some unenlightened soul saw fit to put me in Miss A.'s class for the next school year. At that time in its history the school was extraordinarily strict and I think now that someone took the decision to place me with her because I was seen as a spirited child whose enthusiasm needed to be curbed.

Miss A. had straight iron-grey hair, a beaky nose and fierce, coal-black eyes. She ruled through fear and behaved with a lack of empathy more commonly seen in tyrannical despots than teachers. She was heading towards retirement when I came into her orbit and she seemed to loathe children. There were one or two girls to whom she exhibited blatant favouritism, while the rest of us feared her unpredictability, cutting sarcasm and occasional cruel acts. She possessed an outsize wooden compass, about three feet long, which she wielded with great dexterity in class. In her hands it became a weapon and was employed to hit people on the head, heavily and painfully. One girl was caught bending the spine of a book back and was made to sit for half an hour with her arms pulled tight behind her back in order 'to understand what the book feels like'. She was petty and a bully. Two girls developed anorexia while in her class – the rest of us tried desperately to disappear under the radar and not attract any attention. We were all at that awkward transition between child and adolescent; the last thing we needed was a Pol Pot equivalent wrecking our self-esteem.

For reasons best known to herself Miss A. brought her books to school in a wheelbarrow and would delegate the task of pushing it to any unsuspecting child walking past her on the road leading to the school. One day it was my misfortune to be the one on whom her ferocious eye alighted. I was immediately castigated for pushing the wheelbarrow too fast – in truth, I was desperate to get away from her and put as much distance between us as possible. Reluctantly, I slowed down and walked alongside her, only to be told off for not looking her in the eye. This was because I was fascinated by the incipient moustache growing on her top lip and couldn't keep my eyes off it. This unfortunate prelude to the school day set the tone for the next seven hours. I was delighted when she retired, but wished fervently that she'd gone long before.

In the face of her hostility I retreated into a world of books; I read voraciously to lose myself in other imaginative worlds and to forget the reality of daily school life. Noticing that I was becoming increasingly withdrawn and uncharacteristically quiet, my mother decided to beard Miss A. in her den. Ma was heroic that day and stood her ground against this harridan. She told her, in her quiet understated way, that her behaviour was wholly unacceptable and had to stop. If it didn't, she would have no hesitation in complaining to the headmistress. Miss A. blustered and harrumphed and managed to be both patronising and rude. Her manner towards me, however, subtly changed after that meeting. She chose to ignore me, which was infinitely preferable to the open warfare of previous months. There was a minor setback when she discovered me mimicking her one day, but she mostly left me alone and I regained my equilibrium. The next year my form mistress was Mrs B. who was the complete antithesis – kind, gentle, refreshingly normal and someone who actually liked children. Unsurprisingly, I flourished again.

I had never wanted my parents to grow old and frail, let alone die, but of course the inevitable happened, however much I railed against it when younger. My mother, once so vital and physically active, grew very frail. Reluctantly we decided that she would be safer and better cared for in a nursing home, rather than staying in her own home with carers coming in during the day. It was a big step to take, but carers sometimes failed to turn up and on one occasion she was dropped from the hoist while being put back into bed. These events concentrated our minds and we found a good, local nursing home for her, having visited some real shockers. Throughout all this upheaval my mother was uncomplaining and accepting. She never lost her mischievous streak and would occasionally stick out her tongue at the retreating backs of one or two overofficious staff, much to my delight.

Rachel and I visited every day after work and every weekend; our own lives were deliberately put on hold so that we could spend precious time with her. We knew that she didn't have a great deal of her life left to live and we wanted to make the most of every available moment. We talked and laughed together, read books and newspapers to her and held her hand while she slept, which was often. Ma liked to look smart so she took advantage of opportunities to have her nails painted and her hair done. She had always had very soft skin but now it looked fragile, the veins on her hands standing out like heavily branched small blue trees. When she slept her eyelids were almost translucent and as delicate as grape skin. I used to watch the pulse in her neck, willing it to keep on beating and hoping that she could somehow pull back from the brink and surprise us all. We played music to her, which seemed to give her a lot of pleasure, especially the composers she loved all her life such as Bach and Handel. Her eyes began to assume a distant, faraway look, but they lit up with joy whenever we came into the room. It was heart-breaking. I told myself to note every smile and gesture, every mischievous look, in case it would turn out to be the very last one we would witness. I used to hate leaving her at night, lingering in the room and blowing kisses from the door, reluctant to finally break away. My sister and I felt in limbo much of the time, uncertain about the future. We began to live one day at a time, trying to put the uncertainty to one side and dealing with the day's particular problems. Some days Ma was on remarkably good form and quite chatty, at other times she slept most of the day and was seemingly unaware of us. Occasionally she would surprise us by having a sudden, vivid recall of events from our childhood and teenage years. One afternoon, having been sleepy earlier in the day, she remembered the time I worked on the Christmas post while a student. Unknown to me, she and Pa would watch from their bedroom window as I streaked past the side of the house on my bike and started to pedal energetically up the hill, on the way to the local sorting office. It was six o'clock in the morning, but they got up to watch because they found it amusing to see me race away up the road, head down and legs pumping manically. Ma also remembered the story I'd told her of sorting the post in time to the rhythm of a particular song that was sung every day. The chorus was 'making mad, passionate love' and was sung deliberately slowly, with the Christmas cards and letters being shot into their slots in between the words 'mad', 'passionate' and 'love'. It was like a variation on the great Morecambe and Wise sketch where they prepare breakfast to the tune of David Rose's 'The Stripper'. The story had made my parents laugh a lot at the time and it was lovely to see my mother laughing again now. Laughter transformed her face and she momentarily looked younger and livelier.

The last week of my mother's life was spent in hospital. It wasn't what my sister and I wanted for her but the oxygen saturation in her blood had dropped dangerously low and she needed specialist nursing care. At first she rallied, but then we were told that she had only a short time to live, although the doctors were unable to specify how long. It turned out to be just two days. The last day of her life was a cold, fairly bleak day in February. She seemed particularly tired and couldn't get comfortable in bed; as she was unable to move herself we plumped up her pillows and propped her up against them. As we did so her eyes rolled back in her head and there seemed to be an unfathomable distance between us. For a moment I thought she had gone, but her eyes focused again and she smiled her lovely, gentle smile, the one I used to love as a child when I ran out of school and she was waiting for me. We settled down to our routine of sitting either side of her bed, holding her hands and talking gently to her. A kind family friend arrived mid-afternoon and sat with us; Ma always enjoyed company and seemed to revive a little. The nurse on duty that afternoon came round with a new pill for Ma to take; she explained that it helped to oxygenate the blood. Rachel innocently asked what it was called; the nurse looked distinctly uncomfortable and seemed unwilling to say. Eventually, looking sheepish, she admitted it was Viagra. The three of us round the bed laughed and Ma opened her eyes. She suddenly said, playfully, 'That's why I'm feeling frisky.' We laughed again and hugged her gently; she looked delighted as she'd always enjoyed making us laugh.

Rachel and I decided to leave at about a quarter to six in the evening. It had just begun to snow quite heavily and Ma appeared peaceful. Two nursing assistants made her bed up round her, but she became restless and slightly agitated. I asked her if she was all right but it was obvious that she was beyond expressing herself in any way. Suddenly she began to make a strange, haunting noise and we fetched a nurse. I've always been sensitive to the nuances of people's expressions and knew at once from the look on her face that my beloved Ma had embarked on the unknowable journey from life to death. Rachel and I were asked to wait outside in the corridor while a doctor was summoned. I felt incredibly impotent – my mother was dying and I couldn't do anything to stop the inexorable process.

And so I stood there, anxious and upset, waiting for others to carry out the necessary actions and decide what to do. The doctor – a beautiful Indian woman with a very kind, gentle manner – confirmed that Ma was dying and asked us to go to her bedside to be with her in her last moments. We went straight to her, held her hands, stroked her hair and kissed her. We told her how much we loved her and what a wonderful mother she had been; she may have been past hearing or understanding what we were saying, but it was important to us to say it, a necessary and vital ritual. It was the deepest and most profound rite of passage to be present when the woman who had given me life passed from life to death. She had had a strong Christian faith and I hoped fervently that she had entered eternity and not oblivion. I'm a classic agnostic, wanting to believe but full of unbelief. I love traditional Evensong in a cathedral, particularly the combination of beautiful architecture, liturgy and music, but I suspect I'm seduced by what Archbishop Laud called 'the beauty of holiness'. As I looked at my mother's face and stroked her hair, I wished fervently that Heaven was a reality for her. I couldn't bear to think of her as non-existent, obliterated by death.

When we eventually left Ma's bedside and kissed her for the last time, we stepped out into a world muffled by heavily falling snow. Everywhere was strangely silent, which heightened the crunch of our footsteps as we walked to the car. Both of us were quietly tearful, slightly overawed by the enormity of what we'd just experienced. Suddenly the world did not have our mother in it; we would never again experience her physical presence or be able to hug and kiss her. I looked up at the sky from which so much snow was falling, felt the flakes touch my face with their icy wetness and watched the bright stars for a while. Ever since my teens Thomas Hardy has been one of my favourite writers; I love his novels but his poetry is sublime and, in extremis, I thought of one of his poems now. It is called 'He prefers her Earthly' and in it Hardy describes a beautiful sunset. Whenever I see a glorious sunset or rainbow, especially over the sea along the north Cornwall coast or the hills of Perthshire, both places where we all loved to walk, I think of my kind, wise and humane parents and gain great pleasure from the sheer beauty of the landscape and their presence, somehow, within it.

Chapter 5

UNIVERSITY

THE UNIVERSITY OF Kent sits high on a hill overlooking the city of Canterbury and the magnificent
Canterbury Cathedral. It's a modern concrete and glass
construction and opened its doors to students in 1965. In
2015, therefore, it will celebrate fifty years of existence,
one of the new universities that came into being in the
1960s. It was my home for three exciting years and where
I grew up from a girl to a woman.

When I was a student there in the '70s, four colleges
existed – Eliot, Rutherford, Darwin and Keynes, named
after T. S. Eliot, Ernest Rutherford, Charles Darwin and

John Maynard Keynes. It was a small and very friendly campus comprising just over 3,000 students; relationships between staff and students were excellent and there was a palpable sense of intellectual excitement at lectures, tutorials and seminars. Because it was a new university the courses were wide-ranging and flexible. I read English and American literature and the only compulsory course was Shakespeare, whose plays I had loved at school and came to love even more when studied in greater depth and complexity as an undergraduate. Apart from Shakespeare we could choose what we studied; I did courses in eighteenth-century literature and art, which spawned a keen interest in the artist William Hogarth. One of the first books I bought in my first term was a study of his fine, satirical works *Marriage à la Mode* and *A Harlot's Progress*. I also studied nineteenth-century literature, particularly Charles Dickens, Thomas Hardy and George Eliot. Hardy is an author I return to constantly, not only his novels but especially his magnificent poetry. The poems of 1912–13 recall the courtship of his first wife Emma Gifford forty years earlier, a woman whom he had treated badly and neglected during their marriage. Her death prompted an outpouring of regret and produced poetry that is both outstanding and unbearably poignant.

In my first year I was able to study a multidisciplinary mix of twentieth-century literature, history and philosophy. I concentrated on Virginia Woolf and her stream of consciousness technique, studied the Weimar Republic and the circumstances that brought Hitler to power in Germany, and could choose a European writer to study. My choice was Bertholt Brecht, the German playwright, and I still make a point of going to see any Brecht production that is put on in London. A particular highlight was watching one of my favourite actors, Fiona Shaw, in *The Good Woman of Sichuan* at the National Theatre in 1989. It was heady stuff, spending my time reading and learning, forging new friendships and relationships and learning to be independent and have confidence in my own opinions. I took joy in the books I was reading and the essays I was writing, as well as the many new and interesting people I was meeting. Life was fun, especially being nineteen years old and looking forward to the future with excitement and hope, untainted as yet by cynicism.

I spent my first term in digs in Whitstable very close to the sea. This wasn't an advantage in the winter and I vividly remember writing an essay, swathed in jumpers and scarves in my room, with the rain lashing on the windows and icicles forming on the inside of the glass! In the 1970s Whitstable was a quiet, quaint little place that seemed to have got left behind by the modern world. It had a Dickensian feel to it and looked shabby and unkempt, a far cry from the sophisticated, chi-chi place it is now, complete with oyster bars and restaurants on the beach. It is now upbeat and vibrant, whereas wandering round as a student it felt shabby and ground down, with an air of defeated resignation.

My landlady and her husband were great fun and excellent company; I'd been very lucky in the digs lottery to have ended up with them. Bill and Sue were not that much older than me and had an eight-month-old baby girl, Beth. Bill was a lecturer at the university and sometimes drove me in to lectures in his little red MG sports car. Otherwise I used to get the bus, as Whitstable was twelve miles from the campus, a big disadvantage when trying to get to know people; I always had to leave a party early in order to get the last bus back. The usual conductor on the morning bus wore a very obvious red wig, which slipped a few inches whenever he had to run up and down the stairs to collect fares.

When Sue and Bill were expecting their second daughter, Emily, I got a room in Eliot College and moved all my stuff onto the campus. I had a lovely room overlooking the Cloister Garden and Sue and little Beth came to visit when I'd moved in. I often went back to Whitstable to see them and used to watch Sue performing in the local AmDram group. We still keep in touch nearly forty years on.

Dr Peter Stone was one of the tutors who influenced me a great deal at university. He was quiet and thoughtful and opened up Shakespeare's genius to me in the most vivid and enlightening way. His insights into the work were fascinating, delivered in an understated, almost diffident manner. He was also a man of great courtesy and always made sure that you were comfortable before starting the tutorial. He had rooms in Eliot College that were imbued with the rich, almost heady smell of Disque Bleu cigarettes. He had been a very talented pianist before becoming an academic and often played when his tutorials were over for the day. I would sometimes deliberately walk past his window in order to hear the glorious sounds he made. Rumour had it that he gave up a career as a concert pianist because of the nerves he was prey to before a performance, but I never discovered whether that was true or not. He was kind and considerate and always took time to talk to me about my life and interests, which I appreciated enormously. The comments he wrote on my essays were invariably constructive and encouraging; I wanted to do the very best for him. He died too young, only a few years after I graduated, and I felt a sharp sense of loss when I heard the news. A heather garden was planted on campus in his memory, paid for by donations from friends and colleagues.

My social life blossomed once I was in the thick of things on campus and it was an immense relief not to have to run the length of Giles Lane – unlit and spooky – in order to get the bus at night. Our parties took place in each other's rooms, complete with subdued lighting, scatter cushions and bean-bags. Everyone wore flares – preferably velvet – and platform soles or clogs; nothing seemed to have moved on from Woodstock. We drank cheap plonk, beer and cider, and a lot of people smoked; the mood grew mellower as the evening progressed and the initial intense discussions about the nature of existence and whether there was life after death dwindled into a companionable, zonked-out silence. Cassettes and LPs played music by Kate Bush, who was revered, Tom Robinson and Chicago, particularly the song 'If You Leave Me Now', which was always on repeat.

Tea, coffee and biscuits always followed the Thomas Hardy seminars and Chicago's albums were once again our music of choice. If people came back to my room they were also treated to Grieg, Sibelius and Nielsen, as I had at that point fallen in love with Scandinavian composers. Conversation ranged from the serious to the incredibly silly, stopping at all points in between. There was a hefty seasoning of gossip, most of it benign but with the occasional sharp tang of malice, about who was with whom, who was available and who seemed to rise above the fray, their unattainability adding to their allure.

Tea drinking has always played an integral part in my life, although I'm probably not in the same league as the late Tony Benn in terms of tea consumption. My mother and I shared endless companionable cups of tea throughout my childhood, teenage years and adulthood. We were both quite fussy about the way it was made and insisted on the teapot being warmed before the tea was added. Neither of us liked it too strong nor too weak; praise from Ma for making 'a lovely cup of tea' was praise indeed. My friends knew that any day out with me had to involve a tea shop at some point; at university I developed a taste for Earl Grey and Lapsang Souchong, both of which I still enjoy, although my tastes are eclectic. My friends and I used to joke about what special things we would like added to our tomb, were we of similar status to Tutankhamun! I wanted to be buried with copious supplies of Earl Grey tea, bottles of white wine, a choice selection of football magazines, and the collected works of Thomas Hardy. The Copper Kettle at Chilham was the student tea shop of choice and we often used to drive out there from the campus to indulge ourselves with toasted tea-cakes and scones and jam. I went back there recently and it seemed a pale shadow of what it once was; it had changed its name and felt small and cramped – I had remembered it as being spacious and airy – and had no discernible atmosphere or buzz. Sometimes I think it's best not to return to a much-loved student hangout; the energy, inevitably, is different and the people with whom I shared the experience have gone.

One figure from that time still remains in my memory, because she completely lost her way at university and descended into her own personal Hell, while the rest of us looked on helplessly, unable to stop her precipitous descent. She was bright but started to take LSD, which completely messed up her mind, and her problems were compounded by heavy drinking. In the rare times when she was completely sober she was good company, but it never lasted long. I remember her lurching across campus on a harsh winter's night, each pocket of her duffle coat bulging with a vodka bottle, her uneven progress marked by the clinking of yet more bottles in a carrier bag. One day I was suddenly aware that I hadn't seen her for some time and never discovered whether she had clambered out of the abyss and turned her life around or not. I really hope she made it.

She had been present the night a group of us decided to go to a madrigal concert and ended up in the front row because we'd arrived late and no other seats were free. We were therefore horribly exposed and on view when a collective giggling fit descended on us. The music was delightful and very well sung, but the conductor insisted on telling us the background to each song before it was sung in an idiosyncratic manner and high-pitched voice that soon had us struggling not to laugh out loud. He had a grey moustache not dissimilar to Hitler's and made a little moue with his lips in between sentences, raising his eyebrows simultaneously. We were fascinated by his facial expressions but completely lost it when he talked about the subject of the song resting in the bosom – pronounced 'bosoom' and with the stress on the second syllable – of her lover. The laughter broke through when he made a particularly expressive pout and added 'note the fa la la refrain'. We left in the interval, slightly ashamed of ourselves and knowing that we couldn't withstand another onslaught of pouting and more fa la las.

In my first year at university, I was friendly with a boy whose career path was mapped out even before he started the course. He was going to be an army officer and would enter Sandhurst when he'd graduated; at various intervals he would disappear off to build rafts and learn how to lead men. He was kind and thoughtful, but also seemed to be striving hard to demonstrate that he was a natural leader, decisive and clear-eyed. Each time he returned from these courses he was a little more gung-ho, which held little appeal for me. He had an ancient souped-up car that he drove in an insanely kamikaze manner, roaring through country lanes in the villages near Canterbury as if he was in command of one of the Red Arrows rather than a Ford Anglia. Tight bends were a particular challenge and simply had to be taken on two wheels, with me in the front passenger seat shutting my eyes and praying silently, my foot pressing down on an imaginary brake pedal. When we reached the safety of the campus I would reel out of the car, totter back to my room and refuse to be driven by him again, until he promised not to be such an idiot behind the wheel.

One day he told me he was taking his new girlfriend up to Liverpool to meet his parents. For some reason he chose to drive through the night, fell asleep at the wheel and smashed into the back of a lorry, killing both himself and his girlfriend. People aren't supposed to die at the age of twenty; it seems to go against the natural order of things and when we're that age we think we're immortal. Suddenly he was not in the world, his hopes and dreams brought to a cruelly abrupt end. I remember his kindness and keen wish to be a success in the army; I think he would have made a fine officer.

Eliot College is built in a cruciform shape and has a huge window in the dining-hall, which affords impressive views over the city and cathedral below. Early in the morning the cathedral looked stunning, standing immutable in the limpid light. I often visited the cathedral to immerse myself in its architectural beauty and palpable sense of history. It gave me a sense of serenity, tranquillity and respite from the occasional oppressiveness of campus life, particularly at exam time. Evensong was another oasis of calm, the beauty of the music combining with the aesthetic grace of the building.

The Master of Eliot College asked me if I would be photographed in my room for the university prospectus as a typical student, whatever that was! I agreed and still have a copy – I'm sitting on my bed with a mug of coffee, chatting with my boyfriend of the time, Nick. We both look impossibly young and are wearing the usual student uniform at the time of flared jeans, casual jumpers and desert boots. The posters on the wall depict the well-known beautiful photograph of the young Virginia Woolf and an action shot of the Austrian Olympic skier Franz Klammer. The papers on my desk show that I was in the middle of writing an essay on Jacobean drama. I'd obviously tidied up the room before the photographer arrived; usually books were strewn everywhere along with newspapers and the student paper, then called *inCant*.

My very first radio broadcast took place on UKC Radio, a campus-wide radio station that broadcast on 310 metres, medium wave. I read a news summary from a tiny, cramped room in Eliot College lined with egg boxes, which provided sound-proofing. After the summary I had to introduce a pop music programme called *Wham Bam, Thank You Ma'am*! The small studio, complete with professional equipment, seemed the height of sophistication to me and I revelled in my new role. UKC Radio had a pioneering feel to it, which added to the excitement. It was the UK's first campus radio station and originally, in 1966, propagated its signals along the central heating pipework in Rutherford College.

Nearly forty years on from my time in front of the microphone at Kent, CSR FM is the UK's first student-led community radio station to gain a commercial licence and is a joint venture between the University of Kent, Canterbury Christ Church University, Kent Union and Christ Church Students' Union. It provides a 24-hour, 365-days-a-year service, made possible by the immense dedication and enthusiasm of over 200 student and community volunteers. I went back to the university in November 2013 to receive an honorary doctorate and was lucky enough to meet some of the student volunteers when I was shown round their soon-to-be-completed state-of-the-art Media Centre. I was struck by how committed they were, giving a huge amount of time to the radio station while also studying for their degrees. I loved their enthusiasm and was completely energised by their passion and joie de vivre. It made me wish I was twenty again and setting out anew on life's journey.

The university conferred an honorary doctorate on me in the glorious setting of one of the most beautiful buildings in England, Canterbury Cathedral. It was probably one of the most memorable and special days of my life. I was thrilled that they had chosen to honour me in this way. I spent three very happy years there as an undergraduate and was delighted to go back again when invited to be a trustee of the university's Development Fund from 2003 to 2009.

The day of the ceremony was cool and blustery, with heavy rain in the morning. I woke up excited, but also nervous at the prospect of processing down the length of the nave from the West Door and having to give a speech in front of 2,000 students, academic staff and assorted parents and family members. In spite of the rain the cathedral looked magnificent and excitement began slowly to eclipse the nerves. There was a delicious lunch before the ceremony at which the Vice Chancellor, Dame Julia Goodfellow, spoke warmly about the university and the various ways in which it was prospering. I was then presented with an academic hood and a magnificent framed Giles cartoon from the university's world-class British Cartoon Archive. It's a facsimile of Giles's original artwork published in the *Daily Express* in November

1971 and features Harold Wilson and Ted Heath. The university's crest is inlaid in the frame.

After the lunch I was whisked away to put on my gown and cap for the ceremony. The gown was a striking red velvet and the black velvet cap with tassel complemented it perfectly. Photographs were then taken of me in my finery with my sister, close family friends and the Vice Chancellor and Deputy Vice Chancellor. The photographer was extremely good at putting everyone at their ease and we all look very relaxed and happy in the resulting prints.

After what seemed an age of anxious waiting we were ready to go. As we all walked over to the cathedral the scene appeared medieval and colourful. The many and varied coloured hoods and academic gowns gently flapped in the breeze, while intrigued onlookers stood and absorbed the pageantry. I stood by the great West Door and heard the music start up; I had my very own brass fanfare to process in to. I began the long walk down the nave, preceded by the Director of Development, and it was a moment of pure theatre – the beautiful red gown, the magnificent vaulted ceiling and celebratory music. The pace was deliberately slow and I was aware of faces turning towards me and people craning to get a better look. It was an unusual experience for me, used to the anonymity of the radio studio, to be the focus of all eyes. As I reached the main body of the cathedral, where my family and friends were sitting, I noticed that my sister looked very proud and had tears in her eyes. This moved me greatly as I also had a strong sense of my late parents' presence, like two very loving guardian angels gazing down benevolently.

I received my honorary doctorate about halfway through the degree ceremony. I'd found it fascinating watching the students step up to receive their degrees – so many different faces. Some were diffident and shy, others cocky and a bit brash; one even stopped midway to shaking the Deputy Vice Chancellor's hand, the better to deliver a knowing smile to his doting father, who was busy filming the occasion. Also receiving degrees that day were students from the Circus Space (now the National Centre for Circus Arts) whose degrees are validated by the University of Kent. Their Principal wore a pair of huge, red and blue spotted clown shoes, which nicely undercut the formality of the occasion.

My public orator, Professor Peter Brown, gave a beautifully written – and delivered – speech about my time at the university and the highlights of my career in broadcasting. Some of my exploits elicited guffaws of laughter from the audience and in particular the members of Jubilate Brass who provided the music for the occasion. I immediately felt more relaxed about giving my own speech after I'd received my honorary degree from the Deputy Vice Chancellor, Professor Keith Mander. I'd deliberately kept it fairly short and made it humorous in a bid to stop people from falling asleep, fidgeting and yawning ostentatiously. Fortunately it seemed to work and I was delighted to get a warm round of applause. I felt relieved as I went back to my seat and the rest of the ceremony passed very quickly. Afterwards complete strangers came up to me and congratulated me, which was very pleasant. A tea was laid on and I suddenly felt ravenous and exhausted all at the same time. Sadly, I also had to give my gown and cap back, though I was able to keep my hood. The day had been uplifting, exciting and nerve-racking in equal measure, but it was one that I look back on with great pride and affection. The university gave me a great deal when I was a student there, not least a love of learning and of books, music and art in particular. I've always been very proud of my association with Kent and was enormously honoured to receive an honorary doctorate. The university has always been – and continues to be – a very friendly community and I will never forget their warm welcome for me on that special day.

Chapter 6

BBC –

THE EARLY DAYS

I WAS ENJOYING my time on student radio so much that I decided that I'd really like to get into the BBC once I'd graduated. I listened to Radio 4 a lot and recognised all the newsreaders' voices as soon as I switched on the radio. In my final year I'd read a newspaper article about Radio 4 presentation, which featured Laurie Macmillan – later to be my mentor – and the then presentation editor, Jim Black. What I read lit up my imagination and I decided to write to Jim Black and ask to meet him. I got a response and an invitation to Broadcasting House for a chat and travelled up to London to meet him.

Jim was a complex man and quite difficult to like, although at this initial meeting he was quite friendly and helpful, giving me a lot of information about presentation. We ranged over many subjects and he stressed the importance of curiosity and a well-stocked mind in order to be a good newsreader and announcer. Ultimately it felt more like an interview than a chat, but we got on and I think I acquitted myself well. He told me I had a good, clear voice and even gave me a news summary to read as a parting shot! I was also encouraged to apply to the BBC and to get in touch again if I got in.

I duly applied to become a studio manager and attended three separate interviews in London, keeping my fingers tightly crossed each time that I would get through to the next stage. By now I'd set my heart on getting in and knew that I'd be very disappointed if I didn't make it. I did a lot of preparation before each interview; fortunately, my interests are eclectic and wide-ranging and I think that definitely helped. Interestingly, I don't think I was particularly nervous and remember talking quite happily about all sorts of things and feeling very relaxed. I discussed my talk with Jim Black and my experience with the university radio station; looking back, I think those two factors definitely helped my cause. My third and final interview was with a charming woman who'd worked on *Panorama*, the flagship current affairs television programme, in its early days in the 1950s. We immediately got on well and laughed a lot together; I responded to her warmth and evident good humour and thoroughly enjoyed talking to her. I felt afterwards that I'd done the best that I could and hoped that that would be good enough, although I didn't, however, feel very confident about the outcome.

I learned that I'd got into the BBC on the last day of my finals and the news gave me an enormous boost – the three and a half hours of my Shakespeare paper sped by and it was soon time to relax completely and have a lot of fun, free from the burden of revision and the stress of exam fever. I had a job to go to – one of the few in that fortunate position – and it was a job that I'd wanted and hoped for. I often wonder what I would have done if I hadn't got in; I was interested in acting, arts administration and publishing and might have pursued those options if I hadn't been successful with the BBC.

I joined the BBC in October 1978 as a studio manager. Twenty-four of us were on the same course, fresh out of university and eager to have a good time. We were to be taught the basics of all aspects of radio production, recording technology and tape editing. In those pre-digital days we were forever opening boxes containing huge spools of tape, lacing them up on vast tape machines, recording and then editing. The latter was done by marking the tape with a special chinagraph pencil, cutting with a razor blade, pulling it through and across the spools until the next mark was found, cutting with a razor blade again and then splicing the two ends together with thin white sticky tape. It was a badge of honour to edit as seamlessly as possible and never to leave in an extraneous breath! After a few months I became surprisingly swift and deft and really enjoyed the whole process, even when under pressure against a tight deadline.

The tape machines, manufactured by the Leevers Rich company, were especially cumbersome and unwieldy. When lacing them up with tape they seemed to take on a mind of their own and actively work against you. The tape would often stretch and you'd have to start the whole process all over again. They were particularly ugly, as if designed by an architect of the Soviet Realist school, and were pale green in colour; it was the type of shade that was much in vogue during the 1950s. In idle moments I imagined writing a piece of romantic fiction called *Love on a Leevers Rich*. In truth if you'd made love on one of those machines you'd have been cut to ribbons by the sharp edges of the spools and the various extruding lumps of metal. It was generally recognised that if you could edit on one of those monstrosities, you could edit anywhere.

That was the practical reality but first we had to learn the theory. We sat in various lecture rooms in Broadcasting House learning about sound balance, mixing units and stereo pan-pots. I sat next to a girl called Hilary — we became good friends and soon discovered we were equally unenthused by sound waves and azimuth error!

During particularly boring, turgid lectures we would write jokes and rude comments in the margins of our notepads and pass them to each other. We became adept at smothering our laughter and keeping a straight face.

It was always a treat to be let out of the lecture room to do some practical work. We were unleashed on Oxford Street armed with Uher recording equipment to ambush unsuspecting passers-by and record vox pops. Hilary and I decided, somewhat perversely, to head for the Damart shop and discover why people were buying thermal underwear. They were understandably reluctant to talk to two overly enthusiastic girls who plainly didn't have much clue what they were doing. Our great coup came, however, when we bumped into the actor Derek Guyler. After an initial reluctance to explain why he was buying thermal longjohns, he took pity on us and chatted away happily. We returned triumphantly to Broadcasting House armed with our 'celebrity' vox pops. One of our fellow trainees hadn't been so successful. She'd opened her purse on the street, revealing two razor blades. A sharp-eyed policeman had spotted this and it took her ages to convince him that they were used for her work and not as offensive weapons.

For the first two months of our training our time consisted of lectures, practical work and parties! It was like an extension of university life – making new friends, doing a bit of studying and making the most of living in a vibrant city. There were plenty of social gatherings in pubs near Broadcasting House and trips to the theatre, concerts and art galleries. We were young and relatively free of responsibilities, intent on having a good time.

After eight weeks, we were sent to either Bush House or Broadcasting House to work as trainee studio managers (SMs). I went to Bush House first and found it stimulating, quirky and quaint. We had an extraordinary introductory meeting with a woman who had stepped straight from the pages of a Barbara Pym novel. Josephine was a rather fey character who hummed little ditties to herself as she flitted from her office to the SMs common room, amending our work rotas and constantly giving us little pep talks in her cut-glass accent. I imagined her going home to a small flat of decaying gentility, drinking tea from a Spode china tea set and daydreaming about the ambiguous charms of the curate from the parish church down the road.

At our meeting with her she exhorted us to be ambassadors for the BBC as we worked with the United Nations of foreign-language programme sections. Unbelievably she advised us to wear clean underwear every day and to use deodorant. Undeterred by our sullen silence, she ploughed on with her lessons in decorum and etiquette. When discussing the emergency button hidden under the desk in each studio she became slightly distrait and flustered. The button was to be pressed if you were at the mercy of a presenter's carnal urges or opportunistic fumbles. She couldn't bring herself to put it in those terms and started to colour delicately. She picked her way through acres of euphemism before triumphantly concluding, 'Do try not to cross one's legs and do it accidentally.' Realising that this could be misconstrued, she swiftly left the room with a delicate toss of the head, leaving behind a hint of stephanotis. I don't remember anyone ever having to resort to this safety option, although some of the men fancied themselves as dashing Lotharios and it was therefore a relief to know that the button could be pressed in extremis.

She once walked into our common room, seemed about to say something but thought better of it, did a little skip like a newborn lamb and walked out again. One of the more experienced SMs muttered under his breath, 'Yes Cinders, you shall go to the ball!' I could imagine her stepping out of a magnificent, sparkling carriage to meet her prince, her delicate feet enclosed in glass slippers.

I enjoyed my time at Bush House, meeting the many and varied staff from all over the world who worked there. It was a melting pot of different cultures and languages, and talking to them during long night shifts about literature, music and politics expanded my mind and horizons. I did, however, want to get back to Broadcasting House and domestic radio in order to get into radio presentation, ideally with Radio 4. I was at my happiest taking the role of the presenter in the training exercises we did on our course, always preferring to be on the studio side of the glass rather than in the cubicle fiddling with the knobs.

In that sense being a studio manager wasn't a natural fit, because I wasn't remotely interested in the technical side of broadcasting and couldn't get excited about the intricacies of sound balancing and the finer points of EQ (equalisation). I didn't have a particularly logical mind, but had a vivid imagination and tended to be somewhat dreamy. I was well aware, however, of the limitations of my technical ability and therefore always prepared meticulously and checked everything constantly. This meant that throughout my time as an SM I never perpetrated any technical howlers and no programmes ever fell off air. My heart wasn't truly in it, but I was always conscientious and methodical. I passed my studio manager test without any problems, apart from tripping over my briefcase right at the start. I caught the examiner's eye and we both burst out laughing, which did a great deal to calm my nerves.

I was delighted to be back amidst the art deco splendour of Broadcasting House. Life was good – I was making lifelong friendships and enjoying all that London had to offer. I was certainly having fun.

One of the senior SMs I worked with, Tony, was a hoot and taught me that it was important to enjoy your work. Not long after passing my SM test I worked with him as his 'second pair of hands'; he was on the panel controlling the sound balance and I was responsible for playing taped inserts into the programme we were recording on the bulky tape machines. The programme was *Money Box* and the presenter was Louise Botting. She was plainly a canny financial operator because she swept into the studio with a sumptuous fur coat draped round her shoulders. As she took it off, Tony didn't miss a beat and asked with great politeness whether it would like a saucer of milk. He then managed to look convincingly innocent and Louise simply couldn't tell whether he was being serious or not. It was a delicious moment.

On another occasion he and I were in the canteen getting lunch. The food was notoriously hit and miss and didn't look very inviting, so Tony started making jokes about it. One of the staff behind the counter took umbrage and said to him, 'Are you taking the piss?' He replied with masterly comic timing, 'No, I'll just have the sausages' and walked on. Sadly he died in 2000, after a long-haul flight from Australia, having just worked on the Sydney Olympics for BBC Radio Sport. He was very good at his job and I learned a lot from him. Above all he was good fun and never took himself too seriously. I was always attracted to people like that and did my best to avoid the vain, pompous and self-opinionated, of whom there were more than enough at the BBC.

H30 was like an unofficial common room for SMs. It was a recording and editing channel and adjoined the main studio where *The World at One* and *PM* were broadcast. Everybody seemed to gather there for laughter and gossip, although at key times of the day it could be exceptionally busy and frenetic. Producers would rush through the connecting door after a recorded interview waving a small spool of tape, asking – or demanding, depending on their personality type – that it be edited as quickly as possible. We would then sit with them over a hot tape machine, wielding a razor blade and chinagraph, cutting down a lengthy political interview to a duration of no more than three minutes or so. In those days the producer sitting by my side was likely to be Tony Hall, now the director general, or Kirsty Wark, the journalist and *Newsnight* presenter. Although under pressure, they both managed to be courteous and polite, unlike others who've subsequently sunk without trace. It's telling how people treat those in junior positions. Within the BBC, SMs had and still have a vital role to play in the production and broadcast of programmes and deserve to be treated with respect. It amazed me that certain people felt it was acceptable to be rude and obnoxious; it's such a counter-productive way to behave.

One drowsy summer afternoon, not much was happening either in the world outside or in the confines of H30, and so a plot was hatched. There had been much laughing over a magazine advert's caption and how it could be misconstrued. It was decided to somehow stick it on the back of the girl who was the tape SM on that afternoon's *PM* programme. She was fun and would see the joke. She was also garrulous and could be easily distracted, so it was surprisingly easy to do. Thus it was that she walked around at the back of the studio for virtually the entire duration of *PM* with the words, in large red capital letters, LAY NOW, PAY LATER pinned to her back. A programme producer, finally taking pity on her, told her and it was taken off! She took it in good heart, but nonetheless vowed to take revenge.

Before the advent of computers, an elaborate system of typed hard copy and flimsy carbon copies of cues and running orders was in place for programmes such as the six o'clock bulletin. The run-up to the broadcast was often a fraught half-hour, with news breaking late and the running order constantly changing. The cues were brought to the studio for the Panel SM and me to put in order, and to check what was present and ready to go – and what wasn't. There seemed to be a plethora of flimsy carbon copies that particular day – no good to either of us because they flew off the desk and rack at any hint of movement or rush of air. We often had fun with the names of correspondents in the running order – it wasn't uncommon to see Long, Short and Willey typed out in sequence. On this occasion, with the studio becoming increasingly frenetic and only five minutes to go before the start of the bulletin, Brian – the senior SM – and I only had two hard copies of the relevant cues. Under pressure, Brian called out, 'Listen folks, I've only got a flimsy Willey!' There was a pause, during which everyone in the studio thought 'did he really say that?' And then a great guffaw of laughter. It took us a full ten minutes to calm down and stop laughing and I seem to remember the top of the programme being a bit rackety owing to our mirth.

Throughout my time as a studio manager I was often asked to read out the letters on programmes such as *You and Yours* and *PM*, and at yearly appraisals it was frequently suggested that I move into presentation. It was what I'd always wanted to do, so I needed very little persuading. At the end of my final term at university a lecturer had told me to make my voice my livelihood. I already knew at that point that I'd got into the BBC, so applying to join Radio 4 presentation was very much at the forefront of my mind as a future option. I'd got to know and like some of the established newsreaders of the time – Brian Perkins, Peter Donaldson and Laurie Macmillan – during my stint as an SM and the prospect of eventually becoming one of their number was something I relished.

In 1985 I achieved my ambition and I was taken on as a Radio 4 announcer and later newsreader. The then presentation editor, Jim Black, was on record as saying, 'I have never found a woman who could read the news as well as a man. A news announcer needs to have authority, consistency and reliability. Women may have one or two of these qualities, but not all three.' It's astonishing now to read those words and realise that women were then routinely regarded as second class and inferior, easily dismissed as not being quite up to it. Fortunately, we've come a long way since then, but there's still some way to go and vigilance is needed to ensure our gains are consolidated.

My mentor at Radio 4 was the redoubtable Laurie Macmillan, who became a good friend and remained so until her untimely death over a decade ago. My very first day as an announcer was spent with her on Schools Radio introducing programmes such as *Movement and Music*, where little boys really were exhorted to throw their balls in the air, clap their hands and catch their balls again. Laurie and I spent the day clutching our stomachs with laughter, and I knew I'd found a kindred spirit.

She was an unflappable announcer who kept her feet firmly planted on the ground. Over the years she gave me invaluable advice on how to do the job well, counsel that helped me throughout my nearly twenty-eight years as a newsreader and announcer. She was very hot on checking everything, particularly pronunciations, even if you thought you knew how to say it. That way you were always prepared and unlikely to be caught out by anything. Similarly, she wrote everything down, explaining jokily that she was more than likely to have a brainstorm just as she opened her mouth on air, and completely forget that she was supposed to be introducing *Woman's Hour*. Once when I was with her on Schools Radio she made an uncharacteristic hash of the closing programme credits – or back anno. Afterwards she said, 'Well, that's exactly how *not* to do it – I hadn't prepared enough and preparation is key.'

Laurie was famously straight-talking, but managed to impart home truths with charm and a twinkle in her eye. She had a good sense of humour and was never pompous or self-regarding. Her right eyebrow was a reliable indicator of her mood; it was remarkably expressive, whenever she spotted or suspected bullshit. She could be bracing company and it was refreshing to be with someone who never dissembled. Very sadly, she died from breast cancer in 2002 and R4 was deprived of an excellent announcer/newsreader and I of a vibrant friend and colleague. She would have made a fine presentation editor – firm, scrupulously fair and immune to favouritism or jealousy. Laurie was utterly her own woman and I salute her for that.

When I first worked in the newsroom in 1985 there was a remarkably small number of women working as journalists. What few women there were invariably worked as typists and secretaries. Throw in a small handful of female newsreaders and that was the sum total of women's involvement. Some unreconstructed sub-editors were guilty of casual sexism but could usually be swatted away. As more women entered the newsroom the dinosaurs regularly had their unthinking attitudes exposed and gradually learned to suppress their thoughtless comments, if not actually change their thinking. One or two were more persistent in their beliefs that women were inferior to men. I remember one individual desperately trying to pick holes in my performance when I was a

Family group, summer 1956

Sucking a toy, aged about six months

Family group with Granny, Grandpa and
Aunty Margaret, Christmas 1957

As a baby, with my mother

On the beach, summer 1957

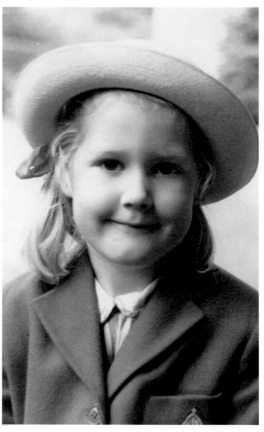

At St Aidan's
school, 1960

With Tim and Stephanie Sherwood, in our garden

Me, aged six

On the beach,
Cornwall, with
Rachel, 1962

Family group in the garden, 1963

With Rachel on the ferry to France, summer 1963

On holiday in
Switzerland, with
my father, 1963

Back at Dover on the
dockside, minus the
windscreen, 1963

With Rachel in
Cornwall, 1964

Dressed up as a sultan for a play
at school, June 1966

With my cousins – and football – at home

Playing the part of John Proctor in
Arthur Miller's *The Crucible* at school

Being photographed drinking coffee
for the University of Kent prospectus

With friends at Kent University
(I am second from the left)

In the Radio 4 continuity studio

**CHARLOTTE
GREEN**

First BBC publicity photo

BBC | ITV | C4 | C5 | DIGITAL | SATELLITE | CABLE | RADIO   LONDON

INSIDE: DELIA'S PERFECT ITALIAN PICKLES

RadioTimes

26 JANUARY–1 FEBRUARY 2002   www.radiotimes.com 85p

"relaxed"

"perfect"

"soothing"

"warm"

"easy"

"velvety"

LOOK WHO'S TALKING

The radio voices that turn you on

How Charlotte Green and Terry Wogan topped our poll Full results page 31

9 770961 887088   05

Cover of the *Radio Times* when I won the award for Most Attractive Female Voice on the Radio; and Terry Wogan won the equivalent for men, January 2002

Another shot taken for the *Radio Times*

With Rachel in north Cornwall

Walking in north Wales

Family group in
Nuremberg, 1993

With my mother in Bonn

With my mother in Cornwall, 2007

Pilgrimage to
the Pips, 2008

Official photograph
after receiving my
honorary doctorate
at the University of
Kent, 2013

brand new newsreader. One of my strengths was my accuracy, so he found it difficult. One day he picked me up on a tiny footling point and I decided I had had enough of his nitpicking. I replied that if that was the only thing he could criticise over the course of a half-hour bulletin, then I was doing pretty well. It was all the more effective because my style is to be calm and low-key in the workplace. When people wrongly assume that you can be walked over, it's good to employ a well-aimed kick and remind them that you can't. Sadly, the BBC is not immune to bullying and some benighted souls attempted to bully me. It wasn't pleasant, but I coped with it by regarding them as losers who were to be pitied rather than feared. Their behaviour was usually motivated by jealousy, so the best response was to carry on doing my job to the best of my ability. They found it infuriating, but that was their problem not mine.

The newsroom in the 1980s was a low-ceilinged space enveloped in a great fug of cigarette smoke, with the windows covered by years of accumulated grime. It was the unhealthiest environment to work in. All day you inhaled other people's cigarette smoke; it was virtually impossible to open the windows, so the smoke settled over the room and never seemed to dissipate. The room was noisy, filled with the sound of clacking typewriter keys. This rose to a crescendo as deadlines neared and the journalists rushed to dictate their copy. Some people had particularly carrying voices and it was difficult to concentrate on your own work while someone was bellowing in your ear about the latest developments in the miners' strike.

Extraordinary as it seems now, smoking was allowed in studios as well. When I walked into the *PM* studio just before five o'clock, Bob Williams and Gordon Clough, who were the co-presenters in the mid-1980s, were usually having a quick drag. On one memorable occasion we all got the giggles just before the start of the programme. There was a relatively new announcer on attachment in continuity who was undone by the programme leading up to the pips coming out early, leaving him with extra time to fill. The motto drilled into me by Laurie was 'always expect the unexpected', but inevitably something conspires to catch you out. This poor boy filled with every trail and filler known to mankind. Eventually, his voice rising an octave higher with desperation and meaning to trail ahead to the six o'clock bulletin, he squeaked 'and in an hour's time you can hear the sick as a cock news'. Bob, Gordon and I caught each other's eye and started to roar with laughter; we weren't quite able to suppress it and the merriment kept bubbling up whenever a tape was played during the programme and we could relax for a bit. Ever since, my family and I have always referred to the six o'clock bulletin as 'the sick as a cock news'!

It was in the same *PM* studio that I narrowly avoided treading on David Blunkett's guide dog, which was half-hidden under the table. The lighting was subdued and as she was a black Labrador she blended in well with the surrounding décor. Aware that I'd sidestepped her at the last moment she gave me a baleful look and then promptly fell asleep. Soon she started a gentle rhythmic snoring, which provided the aural background to my news bulletin. I wondered afterwards if listeners had thought it was me, pulling off the virtually impossible feat of reading out loud and snoring simultaneously.

The third incident that occurred in that studio was when I was introduced by the late Richard Kershaw, then the presenter of *The World Tonight*, as Clive Roslin, even though I was sitting a mere three feet away! I was tempted to say, 'I really must do something about my five o'clock shadow', but thought better of it. I didn't want the listeners to think I was Radio 4's answer to the Bearded Lady. Instead I said that I was actually Charlotte Green 'but what's in a name'. This came out far more acidly than I'd intended – I was amused rather than annoyed and meant to make a joke of it. Richard was remorseful – needlessly because I genuinely didn't mind – and told me that it wasn't personal, as he regularly forgot the names of his children!

Despite its unhealthy atmosphere and some residual antediluvian attitudes towards women, I was very fond of the newsroom in 'old' Broadcasting House. Up until 1998, when we moved to Television Centre (TVC), it was exclusively a radio domain and was therefore small, friendly and personal. When we moved to

TVC everything was bigger, brasher and louder. The space we worked in was like a vast aircraft hangar and the noise seemed overwhelming until you got used to it. The radio desks felt like a small, beleaguered enclave surrounded by the bumptious hordes of television staff. This was John Birt's brave new world of bi-media and we had to get used to it.

Chapter 7

THE LIFE OF
AN ANNOUNCER

PART OF THE duties of a continuity announcer, or 'con', consisted of reading out the credits for drama productions. Sometimes these would be recorded separately, but more often than not I had to step into the studio where the production was taking place and do my bit in front of the cast while they were taking a short break.

One afternoon I turned up for a booking and realised that I was going to have to read out a long list of credits in front of my favourite acting couple, Judi Dench and

Michael Williams. I knew that they were a very unassuming couple as I'd got into a crowded lift with them at the BBC a few months earlier, and noticed how they moved to the back of the lift and did their utmost not to draw attention to themselves. I've become something of a connoisseur of lift behaviour over my years at the BBC and have witnessed much lesser talents than Judi Dench and Michael Williams grandstanding and showing off, as if to remind the lesser mortals present that we were incredibly lucky to be standing cheek by jowl with them. One senior manager was so obnoxious on one occasion that I heartily wished that someone would break wind, giving the rest of us the opportunity to turn accusingly towards the show-off and glare balefully at him! On another excruciating occasion the then chairman of the BBC, Marmaduke Hussey, got in a lift and surveyed us all with the confidence of a man who believes he is intrinsically superior to all those around him. He seemed to think he was addressing troops under his command and barked at us, 'Is everybody happy?' There was a short stunned silence until one brave soul replied, 'You bet your life we are' in a sing-song delivery, as if responding to a Butlin's-style camp greeting. Aware that he was being gently mocked, Hussey's face turned an angry purple and he said no more.

Back in the drama studio Michael Williams was charming and opened the heavy, sound-proofed double doors into the studio, welcoming me in. He had kind eyes and a mischievous smile. I went and stood in front of the microphone to give level and received a lovely smile from Judi Dench. By this point my legs had started to shake at the prospect of having to read in front of two of my acting heroes. Perhaps the anxiety showed in my eyes, because without fuss they quietly absented themselves from the immediate area and went behind some screens. I was so grateful for their sensitivity that I immediately relaxed and the recording went well. Afterwards they reappeared and were charming and friendly. I'd always admired them hugely, but was particularly impressed with their thoughtfulness and kindness towards me that day and have never forgotten it.

Nearly twenty years later I found myself standing opposite the wonderful Bill Nighy in a drama studio, playing myself in a cameo appearance with Bill's character, Charles Paris, the leading protagonist in the Charles Paris Murder Mystery Series *The Dead Side of the Microphone*. The scene had been specially written by Jeremy Front to incorporate me – and funnily enough, it was set in a lift! Charles, an actor and amateur sleuth, has a bit of a fixation about me and my voice, particularly the way I read the Shipping Forecast. He is therefore delighted to bump into me in a lift at Broadcasting House. I also appear in his dreams reading out the Shipping Forecast. It was great fun to do and it was a delight to meet Bill Nighy, another acting hero of mine. He was good enough to sign my script after the recording.

I also played myself in an episode of *The Hitchhikers' Guide to the Galaxy* in 2005 alongside my good friend and former colleague Peter Donaldson. It was directed by Dirk Maggs, who's got a great sense of humour. It was a very relaxed recording and Peter and I spent most of the time laughing and mucking about, although we were serious when it mattered. I always enjoyed working with Peter and with Brian Perkins, revelling in their many anecdotes and funny stories. Brian and I, in particular, set each other off laughing about the foibles or peccadillos of colleagues. I think we both secretly relished being portrayed by two of the talented impressionists on *Dead Ringers*, Jan Ravens and Jon Culshaw. The show was on Radio 4 from 2000 until 2005, but has made a comeback in 2014.

There were some memorable lines from the show, such as 'BBC Radio 4. I'm Charlotte Green. Is that a gun in your pocket or are you just pleased to hear me?' Or 'If satin sheets could talk, they would sound like me.' Another favourite was, 'Radio 4, I'm Charlotte Green, the Home Counties' very own Pussycat Doll.' Brian, as the Godfather of Radio 4, would often say, 'I'm Brian Perkins. At my signal, unleash hell.' Nearly ten years on I still meet people who can quote great chunks from the programme.

Back in December 1988, Laurie Macmillan and I appeared in the *Announcers' Challenge*, a light entertainment show devised and produced by the same Dirk

Maggs who went on to produce the *Hitchhikers' Guide*. A Radio 4 team – Laurie, Eugene Fraser and me – played against a team from Radio 2 and tried to outdo each other with funny anecdotes. I told the story of how, very early on in my newsreading career, I'd contrived to say on the midnight news that the Pope had issued a *condomnation* of all forms of birth control. I just about got myself back on track, only to be confronted with the financial cue that began, 'In the city, rubber prices rose sharply today.' My editor was laughing so much he had to leave the studio temporarily, and I was left to carry on as best I could. I'm delighted to say that Radio 4 triumphed over Radio 2 in both episodes of the *Announcers' Challenge*!

I read the credits for a wonderfully quirky radio comedy, *The Shuttleworths*, from its earliest days in 1993 through to about 1998, when I was chosen to concentrate solely on newsreading. It featured John Shuttleworth – a not very talented singer-songwriter from Sheffield, his next-door neighbour and agent, Ken Worthington, who came last on *New Faces* in 1973, John's wife Mary and other family members and neighbours. All were voiced by their creator, the comedian Graham Fellows.

I thought the programme was very funny, particularly the character of John's wife, Mary, a dinner lady in a local primary school, who was completely unimpressed by John's musical talents. Each programme eavesdropped on John's daily life and was a celebration of the mundane – he liked Wagon Wheels biscuits and a night out at a carvery, and also enjoyed shopping in garden centres. John would often sing whimsical little songs, played – quite badly – on his electronic keyboard. Whenever John got frustrated or fed up he came out with my favourite line: 'Shut up, you wazzock!'

To my delight I was asked to appear as myself in one of the programmes, sitting in a pub with John, drinking a beer, eating some pork scratchings and musing about life! It was quite hard to do as Graham was in Sheffield still putting the programme together. The producer, Paul Schlesinger, and I sat in a studio in London with Paul reading out John Shuttleworth's lines, to which I had to respond. Fortunately, Graham seemed pleased with the result and sent me a T-shirt and other Shuttleworth memorabilia as a thank-you. I've still got the T-shirt, which shows John holding up a red telephone and looking thoroughly bemused.

I always wanted my working life to be fun. Laughter had been an essential part of my childhood and growing up, even in adolescence when life occasionally took on a more melancholy hue. I'm very fortunate to be able to say that my time at the BBC was characterised by a great deal of fun, alongside a few distinctly low points and one or two colleagues whom I would have been very happy to see moving on to pastures new! Apart from the two infamous giggling episodes ten years apart on the *Today* programme, there were many occasions when something in the script made me want to laugh, or ridiculous names suddenly stood out. I once had to read a news story where the name Phyllis Willis kept recurring. It was funny enough the first time I said it, but the more I repeated it the more the name took on a bizarre, surreal quality, until everyone in the studio was desperately blinking back tears of laughter. It happened once again when Mavis Davis made the news. Other favourites included Chastity Bumgardner, whose name I'm convinced was added to a news summary specifically to make me laugh, and the one-time Czech Republic Defence Minister, Josef Tosovski, pronounced toss-off-ski. There is another name that always brought the house down whenever I said it in the warm-up before *The News Quiz*. It belonged to the Turkish investigative reporter Ufuk Uras – try saying it out loud! One spoonerism that I uttered during a news summary I genuinely thought I'd got away with – it was in the sweet old-fashioned days before the advent of social media. Alan Coren, however, heard it and duly repeated it on an edition of *The News Quiz* when I was reading the cuttings. I now know what it feels like to blush in front of an audience of 350 people! I had tried to say 'cross-Channel ferry' but it somehow came out as 'cross-flannel cherry'! Alan seized on this and made much comic capital out of it; I forgave him, however, because his telling of the story was so funny.

Typing errors always made me chuckle to myself when I was sitting in continuity. I once ripped a weather forecast off the teleprinter which stated that there would be heavy SNOT showers in Scotland – what on earth had they done to deserve such an unpleasant occurrence? A script for use in con featured the BUTCH soprano Elly Ameling, who was of course Dutch – thank goodness that didn't get broadcast.

My nickname when I was a child was Charlie or Charlie Girl and some friends still call me Charlie now. My father sometimes called me Lamp-Post because I was tall and thin. As I grew older I wanted to be tall and willowy; I was certainly tall but a little bit of puppy fat prevented me from being willowy. There have been two occasions in my life when that description fitted – when I was in hospital having my appendix taken out and was on liquids for four days, and when I had my wisdom teeth taken out and lived on soup for ten days.

After my wisdom teeth operation my gums bled very badly so my mouth was full of wedges of hard-packed cotton-wool, which were held in place with a huge pink bandage round my face, tied in a big bow on the top of my head. When my father visited me he struggled really hard not to laugh; I looked like a woebegone cartoon character. I managed to mumble, 'Issh not funny', which nearly set him off again. My mouth and gums remained sore and tender for some time, but I was able to go back to work and resume reading without it being too uncomfortable.

This was 1980, the year that a journalist on *The World at One* thought up the nickname that has stuck with me at work ever since. He was interested in all things Italian, and knowing that I liked music, immediately called me Carlotta Verdi. To this day Peter Donaldson – who is sometimes known as Lord Donaldson of the Rolls or Don Pedro – greets me as Carlotta.

I used to like to have a pencil in my hand when I read the news, poised between thumb and forefinger as if I was about to amend the script. Sometimes that's exactly what I did, adding a phonetic spelling for a difficult foreign name or marking a word that I wanted to stress. All these things helped me in my work and so the pencil became an essential prop. If I forgot to take it into the studio with me I felt naked.

Headphones can sometimes seem like an encumbrance, so I prefer to have one 'can' fully on my right ear and the other tucked behind my left ear. The cans now in use at New Broadcasting House grip the head tightly and make my jaw feel restricted. Munch's famous picture *The Scream* is an accurate representation of how I feel when wearing those constricting cans. I also like to have the volume low for two reasons: first because it is more comfortable, and secondly to avoid becoming distracted by the sound of my own voice. If the sound level in the cans is too high, there's a real danger of falling into the trap of listening to your own voice, rather than concentrating on the story you are telling.

Posture is important too – I like to have a straight back and be relaxed yet alert, with my feet planted firmly on the ground. If the seat is too low, you end up slumping into the microphone, which makes it impossible to project your voice properly on air – and it's not good for your back either.

The body language and habits of the editors who sat in the studio alongside me during bulletins could be distracting as well. One always used to sit far too close and invade my personal space; I would tie myself up in knots thinking of polite ways of asking him not to sit on top of me. He also breathed very heavily close to my ear – it was anything but alluring, so I kept trying to edge my seat further away as I was reading. He was prone to loud stomach rumbles and would occasionally burp, forgetting that the microphone was live and it could be picked up. After working with him one morning on the *Today* programme, a listener emailed to ask me how I managed to read a bulletin and burp at the same time. I assured him it wasn't me!

Broadcasting House was home to a large and ever-growing population of mice, but fortunately I never saw one in the studio while I was on air. I'm not quite sure how I would have reacted if I'd seen a mouse wander insouciantly along the floor near my feet. I like to think I wouldn't have let out an involuntary shriek, but who knows?!

When I first began newsreading I experienced all the usual anxiety dreams that occur when you start doing something new. In one particularly vivid dream, all my teeth would fall out as I began to read and tinkle daintily onto the table. I would then be left unable to make any sound other than a whistle, much to the amusement of various shadowy figures lurking at the edges of my consciousness! Variations on a theme were an inability to find the right studio in time, or a script where the pages were forever out of order. Fortunately, these dreams disappeared after a while and no longer plagued me in the small hours of the night.

The continuity studio in the 1980s had a womb-like quality to it, especially late at night or very early in the morning, when I would turn off all the harsh overhead lights and rely on the pool of light from a lamp on the desk. In that intimate setting I would read out the incantatory lines of the Shipping Forecast and say goodnight to the Radio 4 audience. This was an important ritual and I always made a point of signing off with a very personal message. It wasn't sentimental or cloying – both anathema to me – but a simple wish that those listening would have a peaceful night. This resonated with the late-night audience; I received a large number of letters from people who were lonely, either through bereavement or because they were housebound and didn't see many people. That simple wish made them feel included and cared for. It struck me forcibly that Radio 4 provided a vital lifeline for those struggling with isolation and lack of human contact. I consider those few words just before closedown, with just me and a microphone, as some of the most important I ever broadcast.

Chapter 8

NEWSREADING

I ALWAYS LOOKED forward to working a day news shift because the hours were civilised and it gave me a chance to immerse myself in the six o'clock bulletin. This is half an hour of good, clear writing that explains the leading stories of the day in a concise, succinct style. It's the flagship programme of Radio 4 news and it was a pleasure to read. Some days were quiet and calm, the running order decided upon and settled well in advance. Other days were the complete opposite – chaotic, frantic and fraught – with the running order constantly changing and inserts and scripts coming in with seconds to spare.

These bulletins were often a challenge but provided by far the most professional satisfaction. The oft-quoted analogy of the swan is apt here – the reader has to be calm and serene on the surface, but paddling like mad underneath the water.

My day began with a twenty-minute walk to the station, a chance to think about the day ahead and what was likely to lead the news agenda, as well as giving me some physical exercise at the start of the day. The job could be very sedentary so I made distinct efforts to walk around, run up some stairs or generally stretch my limbs throughout the day. If it was a busy news day there wasn't much chance to take a break from the computer screen, although I always tried to make time. I never enjoyed sitting for hours hunched over the screen, forgetting to blink and feeling constricted. A screen break was also mentally refreshing, a chance to think about something else completely unrelated to news. At Television Centre there was always a chance to get outside in the (relatively) fresh air and walk round the main block, which was open to the elements. In the centre was a statue of Helios, the Greek God of the Sun, symbolising the radiation of television around the world. Two reclining figures at the foot represented sound and vision. I would meet friends here and have many conversations about work, play and life itself. The statue was originally a fountain but had to be turned off because it was too noisy and intrusive for staff in the surrounding offices.

My first task was to let the early-morning newsreader go home, usually a little bleary-eyed and weary by ten o'clock in the morning. They would have been up at 3.30 a.m. – horrendously early! – and would have read the bulletins all morning on *News Briefing* and the *Today* programme. Depending on their level of tiredness, my colleagues would either hang around for a bit and have a chat or head for home and bed. If I was taking over from a particular friend we would go and have a coffee or tea together and catch up with each other's news. Because of the somewhat arcane workings of the rota system the newsreaders were the proverbial ships passing in the night, meeting only when beginning or ending a shift. That's why it was such a welcome experience to spend a whole day in each other's company when taking part in the Pilgrimage to the Pips for Rory, of which more later.

Having caught up with friends and colleagues and usually having had a laugh about something or someone, I would read myself in and familiarise myself with the prominent stories of the day. I also read as many of the broadsheets as I could in order to understand as fully as possible the complexities of each story. This is important – if I didn't grasp the salient points of the news story while telling it, then the listener would fail to understand it properly as well. There was a meeting midmorning with the editor of the day and the broadcast journalists working on the bulletins. This was usually a genial affair, with a lot of laughter and dry humour, at which a running order was decided upon for the one o'clock bulletin at the top of *The World at One*. The BBC is inordinately fond of acronyms and any internal email was usually littered with them. A friend and I once spent an idle moment making some up and one of the few that can be published was Seminar for Honesty and Integrity in Television.

Once the running order had been established I could then give free rein to my inner anorak. I liked to be accurate with pronunciations, particularly foreign names and places. When I first began newsreading I was told by Laurie (Macmillan), my mentor, that it was a matter of courtesy to pronounce someone's name correctly, and I've always remembered that piece of advice and tried to be as accurate as possible. Mentioning Laurie has reminded me of my very first news summary in early 1986, in studio 3G at the back of the radio newsroom in Broadcasting House. Sadly, neither studio nor newsroom exists now, but an accurate reconstruction was made for the film *The Ploughman's Lunch*, which was released in 1983. It was written by Ian McEwan and directed by Richard Eyre and portrayed the media world in Margaret Thatcher's Britain during the Falklands War. I remember it for a fine performance from Jonathan Pryce as a devious, opportunistic radio reporter, and also for a marvellously funny and gloriously indiscreet running commentary from the actress Miriam Margolyes, who happened to be sitting behind me in the cinema!

I was in the newsroom at about 1.50 p.m., waiting for Laurie to appear for the summary at two o'clock. I'd been trailing her all day and sitting in on her summaries and one o'clock bulletin, in preparation for my first news shift. I was just beginning to feel vaguely uneasy at her non-appearance when the phone rang. Laurie – in her usual breezy way – said she wasn't doing the summary and would I do it instead. Fortunately, there was no time for nerves, although I do remember feeling slightly queasy as I walked into the studio. To my dismay, my least favourite studio manager was sitting in the control cubicle, waiting to put me and my summary on air. He had an unfortunate habit of wrapping his hands around my backside whenever he got the chance, which thankfully wasn't often. The pips went out at the top of the hour, my microphone was opened and I was on air reading the two o'clock news summary, the first of many during my 27-year career. I don't remember anything about the news content, but do recall that it felt simultaneously like the longest and then the shortest two minutes of my life. When I walked out of the studio, Laurie was waiting in the newsroom, grinning all over her face; she gave me a laconic 'Well done!' and we went off for a celebratory cup of tea.

Soon after I first began reading the news I saw a journalist being half-dragged out of Broadcasting House reception, boozily singing 'Show me the way to go home' at the top of his voice. It was an entertaining sight, but probably not the image that the BBC wanted to project to members of the public waiting in the foyer. In those early days I regularly had to learn to put up with breathing the beer fumes of certain editors as they sat next to me in the news studio. It was like broadcasting from within a beer keg!

The very famous – and very funny – 'The Fleet's Lit Up' broadcast by Thomas Woodrooffe, who was attempting to describe the Spithead Review from his old ship HMS *Nelson* in 1937, is a stark reminder of the dangers of combining alcohol and broadcasting. He'd had some drinks with former naval colleagues before the broadcast, which resulted in such incoherence that he was taken off air within a few minutes. The BBC director general, John Reith, suspended him for a week. Woodrooffe was described – possibly for the first time ever – as tired and emotional!

Some years later the summaries became self-op, which meant that we operated all the equipment ourselves while reading, without the luxury of a studio manager to open the mic and play in the voice piece, which in the 1980s was on tape. I wasn't blessed with a particularly logical mind and also, to be honest, couldn't get that excited by the technology of a radio studio. I therefore took the training seriously – and sometimes asked for extra training – in order to avoid as far as possible committing any howlers live on air. One former colleague got into a terrible tangle putting out the four-minute midday bulletin, which was self-op. I don't quite know how it happened, but each voice piece she played in bore no relation to the cue she'd just read. It made for riveting radio, a fascinating aural equivalent of the Theatre of the Absurd, each mismatch more surreal than that which preceded it. Eventually it all lurched to an end and the continuity announcer picked up sounding stunned.

The World at One is presented by Martha Kearney, whom I'd met some years before when she presented *Woman's Hour*. I'd been asked by the latter programme to have a full body spray-on tan and then describe the experience to Martha a few days later. She's very friendly and approachable and I enjoyed the light-hearted interview. I also enjoyed having the tan and felt vaguely like a film-star for all of forty-eight hours. After that the tan began to wear off and became noticeably streaky on my legs, a rather unattractive after-effect.

The news bulletin on *WATO* lasts about four minutes, so the newsreader makes a very brief foray into the programme and then returns to the newsroom. There's time for a short lunch break before the serious business of the afternoon meeting, held to discuss the running order for the *Six O'Clock News*. Sometimes the top story was so obvious that there wasn't much room for debate. On other occasions there would be a lengthy and lively discussion about the relative merits of each competing story. These meetings were entertaining and good natured; in general the journalists I worked with

in the newsroom were very pleasant and convivial people. They worked hard, wrote well and were graceful
under pressure. I loved my work there, probably because
there was so much laughter and good humour, in spite
of the appalling stories that we were occasionally dealing with. One of the first female assistant editors in the
newsroom had a good sense of humour and if we ever
caught each other's eye over something funny, we had
to work hard to suppress the mutual amusement. Her
job involved sitting next to me in the studio – always
dangerous given the likelihood of collapsing into mirth
– handing me scripts and working out the timings, so
that we finished at 6.30 p.m. precisely. One evening we
were particularly rackety and I'd had to resort to reading with my hands covering the sides of my face like the
blinkers of a horse. We ended the bulletin on the dot of
what we both thought was half past six and started col-
lecting our scripts. Claire looked again at the clock and
went very pale; I looked enquiringly at her and she said,
'We've come out a minute early.' It was then we realised that continuity was stoically filling the extra time
with all sorts of trail material. Profuse apologies were
offered to con and accepted and we moved on. Recently
we bumped into each other by chance in a lovely country pub, both of us in the middle of a long walk in the
Chilterns. It was good to see her again and virtually
the first thing we remembered was our ever so slightly
short six o'clock bulletin!

The really good assistant editors made sure that I had what I needed before going on air – the headlines and first cue, as well as ensuring as far as possible that I was able to see scripts that were coming in during the bulletin. It wasn't a given that the headlines and top script would be there in front of me as Big Ben began to chime. If no hard copy was forthcoming I would read off the computer screen; in the early days of computers this could be tricky as the screen was liable to freeze or the text to disappear altogether. I remember listening to a Radio 4 news bulletin long before I joined the BBC and hearing the newsreader pause during the headlines to say, 'I'm sorry, I can't read my editor's handwriting.' A line must have been written in at the last minute in great haste and was illegible. Usually, however, I would have the relevant scripts, although this didn't necessarily mean that the headlines would be read out in the order they were printed on the page. On more than one occasion the order was changed at the very last moment, with my editor having to point at the headlines he wanted first, second and third. It certainly kept me alert.

At 6.30 p.m. the red light in the studio would go out, indicating that we were off air, and we would walk back to the newsroom for a short debriefing about the bulletin. This was held in all circumstances, whether there had been high drama or a smooth, calm progression through the stories. I was now free to go and would usually have a chat with whoever was reading the late news before I headed home. A rare free evening beckoned and I was keen to make the most of it.

The World Tonight is a considered, thoughtful current affairs programme, which I always try to listen to if I'm at home. When I was newsreading, the main presenters were Robin Lustig and Ritula Shah. They're both charming and very good company and I always looked forward to joining them in the studio to read the ten o'clock bulletin. One evening another journalist was presenting the programme and referred in his preamble to the prospect of George W. Bush leaving office and another Bush family member running for President. He intoned, 'Is there room for another Bush in the White House?' at which the assistant editor beside me started to snigger. I then had to dig my nails into the palm of my hand in order to get through the first cue, not an easy task when a colleague is losing control and stuffing his fist in his mouth. Fortunately, neither of us tipped over the edge and the rest of the bulletin ran smoothly.

I had one hairy experience on a late shift when I decided to go to the loo at the last moment before the midnight news. I knew I wasn't really allowing myself enough time; I thought this was preferable, however, to plaiting my legs for thirty minutes. All was going well until the loo door jammed and I couldn't get it open. I banged it, shook it and even tried to force it open by flinging my body at it. The door wouldn't budge and my skin began to feel prickly with fear and rising panic. I was beginning to despair, thinking I'd forever be known as the announcer who got stuck in the loo. Unbelievably, somebody actually came into the cloakroom at this point and I explained my predicament through the door. Between us we somehow got the door open and I raced to the studio; the editor wasn't really fussed and just assumed I was playing it very cool! The headlines were read rather slowly and deliberately that night in order to help me get my breath back. After that incident I never cut it quite so fine again.

The late shift had an altogether different feel to it. Sometimes it would loom over the earlier part of the day like a dark cloud; I would always have at the back of my mind the knowledge that I had to be at work at 4.30 p.m., and tried to fool myself into thinking it was a day off. There was also the danger of doing too much before the shift started and feeling exhausted by the time the midnight bulletin began. On the plus side, late shifts meant that I got to work with Eddie Mair on the *PM* programme, which was always entertaining and slightly anarchic. Eddie has the enviable ability of being able to say something really funny while keeping a completely straight face; half the time I never really knew whether he was being serious or not, but the programme was wonderfully exhilarating to be a part of and to listen to. He brings a lovely subversive element to it, which makes it compulsive listening.

If the six o'clock bulletin could be likened to a

classical music concert with full symphony orchestra, then the midnight news was a jazz concert – intimate, with the lights down low and a laid-back vibe. It was usually a relaxed read with little of the urgency of the six o'clock and I deliberately kept the lighting very subdued to match the mellow mood. The bulletin was an excellent round-up of the whole day's events, including sports news and a look at the first editions of the newspapers.

Once safely home at the end of the shift it always took me at least an hour to wind down before going to bed; my mind would be buzzing with all the stories I'd been reading about in the midnight news. Sleep was a bit patchy and all too soon I would wake and ease myself gently into the new morning.

The one aspect of my job that I came to loathe was the shift pattern, in particular night shifts and early shifts. When I left the BBC in early January 2013, I remember saying to myself, 'No more disrupted sleep, no more feeling of permanent jet lag and no more wandering around the house with a small black cloud hanging over my head, thinking I've got to be up at 3.30 a.m.'

I didn't function particularly well in the early mornings – frankly, who does? It was impossible to relax and sleep deeply, because I was too aware of having to get up as soon as the insistent alarm clock went off. I usually found myself waking once or twice an hour, convinced it was time to get up and face the fray. This meant that by the time I really did have to get up I was bleary-eyed and feeling distinctly groggy. The consequences of over-sleeping, however, were too grim to contemplate and so I was stuck with this wretched pattern of light sleep and wakefulness. I sometimes used to go through agonies if the taxi that was coming to collect me was late. I would stand at the bedroom window peeping through the curtains, willing the beam of the headlights to appear round the corner to show it had arrived. It didn't help that, in the days before Satnavs, my house was quite difficult to find, right on the spine of the A–Z page.

In the latter years of my time at the BBC the news-readers didn't work a full overnight shift, but instead got up at approximately 3.30 a.m. to do the early shift, which included the *Today* programme. Earlier in my career we finished with the midnight bulletin at 00.30, had some restless sleep until 5 a.m. on site or nearby, got back into the BBC at 5.30 and then – ideally! – sounded rested and alert on air at 6 a.m. Neither shift enabled you to be at your best on the *Today* programme, but we all did a very good job of coping and disguising our weariness.

Over the years we stayed in some bizarre and eccentric places for our precious few hours of so-called rest. They were never salubrious, comfortable or conducive to sleep. At one time we were put up in a BBC hostel a short walk away from Broadcasting House. One night as I came out of the building a rather creepy man waiting by the main door said he was an intimate friend of mine. I replied that I didn't know him and went straight back into the building. I found two of the tallest, burliest journalists in the newsroom and they kindly escorted me round to the hostel. After that slightly unnerving experience there was no shortage of gallant colleagues willing to walk with me. I think they were glad to take a short break from the newsroom!

I was once accompanied by Brian Perkins, who was also staying overnight. For some reason we were refused entry by a fretful concierge, who kept saying querulously, 'No, no, you're not who you say you are, you're not on my list.' It took us a long time to persuade him to let us in; we were even reduced to saying 'Radio 4' out loud in a bid to convince him.

The worst accommodation I stayed in overnight by some way was a small hotel in Shepherd's Bush, although the word 'hotel' distinguishes it in a way it didn't deserve. It soon acquired the nickname 'The Bosnian Bordello'. I was convinced it was a knocking shop as every time I stayed there the sounds of vigorous rutting could be heard through the extremely thin walls. It was seedy, dirty and depressing and I don't know why I put up with it for so long. There was no lock on the bedroom door so I shoved a chair under the door handle for some scant feeling of security. I never slept well there, unsurprisingly, and was always fearful of a fire breaking out, especially as cigarette smoke used to waft into the room from a neighbouring bedroom.

It was potluck whether you actually got into the hotel

in the first place. We all had a key to the front door but
the lock was maddeningly imprecise and you could spend
an increasingly frantic ten minutes trying to get the door
open. I was nearly in tears of frustration one night, thinking I would have to spend a sleepless few hours on the
doorstep. When I looked down I spotted an enormous
rat step nonchalantly over my feet and go on its way; it
was the last straw and I complained that the BBC was
failing in its duty of care.

The next overnight accommodation we moved into
was better, but still had no lock on the door. The room was
large and had a bathroom built underneath it, which could
be reached only via a steep spiral staircase made of metal.
The descent was so precipitous that I couldn't help feeling that one of the small band of newsreaders who stayed
there overnight would, one early morning, groggy after
a few hours of disrupted sleep, plunge to the bottom of
the staircase with possibly fatal consequences. I once
tripped up the wretched thing, bashing my knee on a
metal stair, and then had to plough through a three-hour
Today programme with an increasingly painful, swollen
and throbbing joint. Eventually our shifts were altered,
we no longer worked full overnights and got to sleep in
our own beds before early starts. The problem of intermittent, unrelaxed sleep was never overcome, however,
and getting up at 3.30 a.m. remained the one time when
I questioned the wisdom of working as a newsreader.

Chapter 9

MEMORABLE EVENTS
AND BROADCASTS

IN THE LATE 1980s in the newsroom at Broadcasting
House there was a time when journalists would call out
'Nobody get on a plane tonight, Charlotte's doing a night
shift' as I walked in to start an overnight shift. This black
humour – typical of the newsroom – arose because I had
been on duty the night Pan Am flight 103 crashed over
Lockerbie on 21 December 1988, destroyed by a terrorist
bomb. Just over two weeks later I was also on duty when
the Kegworth air disaster occurred on 8 January 1989.

The plane was attempting an emergency landing at East Midlands airport, but crashed onto the embankment of the M1 motorway near Kegworth in Leicestershire.

In both incidents there were inevitably fatalities and serious injuries. At Kegworth forty-seven people died, while at Lockerbie all 243 passengers and sixteen crew members on board were killed and eleven people died on the ground in the town of Lockerbie itself. The latter remains the deadliest aviation incident in the UK. When news of the crash first filtered through to the newsroom I had to read a news flash stating that the plane had crashed, but that there had been only one fatality. Sadly the horror of the accident slowly unfolded and it became apparent that a great many people had lost their lives. Awful details began to emerge of dead bodies still strapped into their seats, discovered on farmland and hanging off the roofs of buildings. These details were not broadcast, but made a big impact on me as more and more information came in. I distinctly remember the contrast between the Christmas decorations and the sparkling Christmas tree lights in the newsroom and the sober, subdued attitude of the journalists. We'd all been jolly when the shift started, enjoying the run-up to Christmas, but now people were focused and serious. For once the banter had stopped and the newsroom, usually so noisy and hyperactive, was unnaturally quiet.

When difficult stories like this break, the newsreader has to keep his or her natural emotional responses in check. I was pretty upset by the horrendous detail that was emerging from Lockerbie, but knew that it was essential that I kept that response hidden in order to read in a calm, considered way. It would have been completely inappropriate to have descended into sentimentality or mawkishness. People want to hear the news read intelligently so that they can understand the salient points, and I always aimed to read it in an authoritative and measured way.

On the Thursday morning after the Lockerbie crash the *Today* programme reported from the scene. John Humphrys was there and did an excellent job, setting exactly the right tone. He elicited illuminating responses from those living in the town, but was never intrusive. I had slept very badly in the short break I got between the end of the midnight news and the start of the *Today* programme. My mind was fizzing with the enormity of what had happened and the horror of the images that had been revealed to us in the newsroom. I also couldn't stop thinking about the many families whose lives had been shockingly ripped apart by the abrupt death of loved partners and family members. These feelings had to be hidden once the *Today* programme was underway and I did my best to achieve a synthesis of authority and warmth. Sentimentality is something to be avoided, but there is definitely a place for empathy. Even now, if someone mentions Lockerbie, I'm immediately transported back to that night shift in mid-winter and the tumble of emotions I felt as the night progressed.

I love walking in Kew Gardens and frequently visit the memorial to Pan Am flight 103 that was put up there. The plane's flight path took it over Kew and the wooden bench built around the vast girth of an oak tree near the lake specifically remembers the names of the flight crew who perished. It is simple yet incredibly moving.

In March 1987 the Zeebrugge ferry disaster occurred and I was faced with my very first big disaster. Again I was on a night shift and the story developed into something terrible and tragic. The *Herald of Free Enterprise* was a roll-on roll-off ferry that capsized moments after leaving the Belgian port of Zeebrugge, killing 193 passengers and crew. The bow door had been left open and the sea flooded the decks. As with Lockerbie, the human stories were unbearably poignant and made the most impact. Most of the victims were trapped inside the ship and died of hypothermia. Andrew Parker was awarded the George Medal, one of the highest civilian awards for gallantry, for his actions that night. He was 6ft 3in and used his frame to form a human bridge; twenty people managed to clamber across him. Sadly he witnessed behaviour where people pushed others out of the way in order to save themselves. I slept very poorly that night too, thinking of those trapped inside a pitch-black ship on its side, freezing cold and surrounded by panic and fear. Rushed into eternity or oblivion, depending on your belief – or lack of belief – in an afterlife. The next morning it was imperative to tell the story clearly and authoritatively, keeping my own emotions and feelings in check. It was a frenetic night shift and I was exhausted when I got home.

There have been many other occasions where the emotional impact of the news story has been considerable. I read the special one-hour-long six o'clock broadcast on the first day of Operation Desert Storm. The first Gulf War lasted from 2 August 1990, when Iraqi troops invaded Kuwait, until 28 February 1991. I was aware of the historical significance of what I was reading and felt a weight of responsibility to read clearly and intelligently. I think all those involved in the bulletin would have been disheartened if we had known then that there would be another outbreak of war in the region in 2003.

I met a former senior news editor, Andy, at a BBC gathering recently and he reminded me that we had been doing the midnight news together one night when all the lights went out. Unfortunately, the emergency generator failed to kick in and we had to abandon the studio. We were trying to make our way towards a studio in the inner part of Broadcasting House, where the lights were working. The corridors, however, were in complete darkness and we had to hold hands and feel our way along the walls in the pitch black.

The two of us also worked on a special, extra-long bulletin during the evening of the terrible events in New York and Washington on 11 September 2001. Four coordinated terrorist attacks were launched by al Qaeda that day, killing almost 3,000 people. The planes were deliberately crashed into the twin towers of the World Trade Centre, which both collapsed causing enormous loss of life. A third plane was crashed into the Pentagon, while the fourth aircraft was targeted at Washington, DC. This crashed into a field in Pennsylvania, after its passengers – in an act of great bravery – had attempted to overpower the hijackers.

I first became aware of what was happening while out shopping before going in for my late shift. A crowd had gathered outside a shop selling televisions and other electrical equipment. I could just make out footage of a plane flying into a building, and thought it was a disaster film. I couldn't understand why it was attracting such a large crowd and was about to move on, when someone told me what had happened. I immediately went home and got ready for work. I rang the newsroom to say I would be in early as I knew they would be very busy and might need an extra pair of hands before my shift formally started.

The television feeds in the newsroom showed that something shocking and brutal had taken place, a stark example of man's inhumanity to man. I was very grateful to be working with Andy – he was calm and methodical, unflustered by the apparent chaos around him, made good decisions and kept me fully informed of last-minute changes. We worked well together. By the time we were about to put out the midnight news, we were both tired, but determined to broadcast as good a bulletin as we were capable of producing. I found the entire shift a sobering experience, particularly the terrible details of what emerged throughout the evening. It felt as if an imaginary line had been crossed and the world could never go back to the way it was before. The impact of the attacks has been enormous and far-reaching, both geographically and on society and culture.

I was also on duty on 7 July 2005, the day of the London tube bombings. I managed to get into work by taxi and was then part of an extremely efficient news operation mounted by the newsroom for Radio 4. Their work was superb and we put out an extra-long bulletin at six o'clock that was a masterpiece of good, clear writing and reporting. It rightly won a Sony Gold Award the following year. The studio was fairly chaotic and frantic and I had to sight-read a lot of the scripts. Four suicide bombers and fifty-two civilians were killed and over 700 people were injured. It was terrible and shocking, not least because the attacks took place just a day after London had celebrated winning the bid to host the 2012 Olympics. I remember the bulletin because of the stories of horror and heroism it told; the dreadful randomness of the attacks and the magnificent way in which people responded. I also recall being very focused and concentrated throughout the duration of the programme. Live reports came in at staccato speed from all round London; I was reading scripts sight unseen and the whole hour seemed to pass in a matter of seconds, so deep was my concentration. It's what athletes call being 'in the zone' and was probably the nearest I've ever come to achieving that state. This helped me when I was told to evacuate the studio at very short notice because of a credible bomb threat. I made a short announcement and continuity took over – a difficult task for the continuity announcer with no warning. We moved to a studio further inside TV Centre that was deemed to be less vulnerable and resumed the bulletin. It was an exhausting, stressful day but I was fortunate to be able to go home to my family who were all safe. So many people suffered that day in so many different ways; the carefree and joyous mood of the previous day – when we learned that the Olympics were coming to London – had been irrevocably shattered.

One of the rare times in my career when bulletins were given over to positive, uplifting news occurred when demonstrations in East Germany, and people fleeing the GDR through open borders from Hungary to Austria, eventually prompted the fall of the Berlin Wall on 9 November 1989. This was a time of immense joy and celebration, with East Germans – delight and disbelief mingling on their faces – flooding through the open border crossings into West Berlin to be greeted by West Germans proffering flowers and champagne. It was heart-warming and uplifting and I relished reading the bulletins that covered this highly significant news story.

Twentieth-century German history fascinated me. In my first year at university I had studied the period from the creation of the Weimar Republic to the rise of Nazism, as well as the life and work of Berthold Brecht. This led to further reading about the foundation of East Germany and the building of the Berlin Wall. On a number of occasions I'd stood on the viewing platforms that overlooked the wall on the West Berlin side. It was a forbidding sight. There was a chilling death strip that was covered with sand or gravel; anyone stranded there would be an easy target for the armed guards in the watchtowers. As soon as anyone popped up on the viewing platforms the East German guards swivelled round and fixed their binoculars on them. I was tempted to wave but thought better of it. They were very young and obviously incredibly bored. I remember thinking that the wall would never come down in my lifetime; just three years later I was reading about its demise on Radio 4.

On one visit in 1985, my sister and I visited East Berlin for a day. It took forever to pass through Checkpoint Charlie – the coach we were travelling on was minutely checked with large mirrors being placed under every seat. Passports were scrutinised closely and occasionally taken away to be checked even more thoroughly. This happened to mine, presumably because it showed that I worked for the BBC. The guards were dour and unsmiling and seemed to take no pleasure in their work. Everything was checked and rechecked obsessively; they appeared to be suffering from a collective paranoia that led them to distrust everything. I wondered whether they went home at night and managed to throw off the cloak of defensiveness and suspicion, laughing and smiling with family and friends. Or did the suspicion creep insidiously into everything, permeating their closest relationships? We know now that husbands spied on their wives and vice versa, with even the most innocuous detail being relayed to East Germany's secret police, the Stasi. A brilliant film was made in 2006 by Florian Henckel von Donnersmarck called *The Lives of Others* (*Das Leben der Anderen*), which portrayed the monitoring of an East Berlin playwright and his girlfriend by the Stasi. It's a quietly powerful film depicting a moral and political quandary with great subtlety. The Stasi officer is transformed from a hard-nosed servant of the state to someone who cared for the fate of the people he was watching, to the point of protecting them.

Finally our coach made it into East Berlin and we were joined on board by our guide, a trusted party apparatchik called Frau Schwarzkopf (Mrs Blackhead!). We were taken to Treptow Park to view the massive and hideously ugly Soviet war memorial and she regaled us with tales of the heroism of the Red Army and the Soviet Union's great love and support for the people of East Germany. She couldn't tolerate any criticism of the East German regime and ignored any difficult questions from a group of sceptical Americans. Everything looked dull and dreary, all muted tones and a complete lack of bright colour. The buildings were unkempt and dirty, with trees and bushes growing out of the roofs. The people we saw seemed bowed and resigned to living in this oppressive, monochrome world. Frau Schwarzkopf told us that East Berliners loved to relax in cafés with their families. We were taken to one in the park and soon realised that our group was to sit separately from the locals on another floor. There was to be no communication between East and West.

In the 1990s my sister had a posting to the British embassy in Bonn and later Berlin when the seat of government moved there. This led to many fascinating visits, retracing the site of the wall, using maps of the time. There's little physical evidence of the concrete structure remaining, but three long sections are still standing. It still makes me shudder to this day – 136 people died trying to escape, often shot by the guards in the watchtowers. One would-be escaper was shot and left to bleed to death on the death strip, in full view of the West. The Checkpoint Charlie Museum has many examples of the ingenuity of those who were desperate to gain their freedom. Long tunnels were dug under the wall, hot air balloons were used, as well as microlights and aerial wires. My sister has a fragment of the wall, complete with its certificate of authenticity, given to her when she was at the British embassy. On 13 August 2011 Germany marked the fiftieth anniversary of the beginning of the building of the Berlin Wall by East Germany. Those who died attempting to escape to the West were remembered and honoured.

It was another momentous day in Germany's history on 9 November 1989. I would love to have been in West Berlin that night, celebrating with the East Germans as they streamed through the border crossings, intoxicated with the novelty and excitement of freedom. To be part of the coverage of these extraordinary events on the BBC was, however, the next best thing.

Chapter 10

TODAY

THE CLOCK TICKED agonisingly slowly round towards
3 a.m. I had been wide awake for forty-five minutes,
having got to bed a mere hour and a half before. I was
sleeping in The Langham, an imposing building across
the road from Broadcasting House, which is now The
Langham Hotel. My colleagues and good friends, Peter
Donaldson and Brian Perkins, had teasingly told me that
the building was haunted, the night hours punctuated by
clunking noises redolent of Tudor knights in armour.
Knowing the precarious nature of the plumbing there, it
was far more likely to be the pipes, but my imagination

nevertheless began to run away with itself. I knew too that a mischievous Radio 2 announcer, James Alexander Gordon, who wore callipers because of childhood polio, deliberately used to drag his leg as he walked along the corridor, spooking one or two colleagues susceptible to the notion that The Langham accommodated other-worldly phenomena!

My stomach churned and my brain was hyperactive, feverishly playing and replaying a number of slightly surreal images in my mind's eye. I was in the middle of a long overnight shift and in just over two hours would be preparing to make my newsreading debut on the *Today* programme, Radio 4's flagship news and current affairs show. Hence the trepidation and spasmodic sleep. It was 1986 and I was about to meet Brian Redhead and John Timpson for the first time.

When I read my first bulletins, summaries and newspaper reviews on the programme that morning, I had no inkling that I would be privileged to sit in the *Today* studio in one of the 'best seats in the house', observing the myriad politicians, distinguished guests from the arts and sciences and other contributors who all had a compelling story to tell, for the next twenty-seven years. The leading political players from the '80s, '90s and noughties sat at the famous U-shaped table and engaged in gladiatorial combat with *Today*'s talented presenters, all of whom excelled at holding wily political operators to account.

The *Today* programme is required listening for politicians, journalists and other opinion-formers. It regularly garners Radio 4's largest audiences and has come to be regarded as a programme that should never be missed. It's an agenda-setter, with heavyweight political interviews and a serious tone, albeit leavened with humorous features and the natural quick-wittedness of the presenters. This is all a far cry from the amiable low-key style of *Today* from the late '50s to the mid-'60s. It was described by John Timpson as 'not so much a programme, more a way of telling the time'. Its main presenter at that time, Jack de Manio, was notorious for being incapable of reading the clock and his gloriously gin-soaked voice would regularly get it spectacularly wrong. He's remembered in my family for not being able to say the word 'organism'; three times he tried it and each time it came out as orgasm, much to the delight of my sister and me, agog in our school uniform at the breakfast table!

John Timpson and Brian Redhead were the presenters on my first morning in 1986. John was quiet, reticent and pleasant; a self-contained man who was noted for his light-hearted 'ho ho' items, which acted as a counterpoint to the serious pieces. Brian was a complete contrast – ebullient, bumptious and quite unabashed in regaling you with stories of his many, well-deserved broadcasting triumphs. He was also kind and avuncular and reminded me of the rosy-cheeked, cheery figures who could be found in the seventeenth-century Dutch paintings of Jan Steen. Within minutes of meeting me he was showing me photographs of his cat, advising me to choose someone kind as a life partner – excellent advice – and talking about music and books. He was stimulating company, the master of the witty quip and sharp one-liner, and I grew fond of him. Wherever he went he was always humming to himself, a man at ease with himself and the world. He loved his job and clearly relished the cut and thrust of live broadcasting. The only time I saw him subdued and unusually quiet was during one of his last appearances on *Today*. He was obviously in pain and confided to me that he didn't feel at all well. He took leave from the programme in early December 1993, expecting to be back after Christmas, but died in January 1994. I was on duty the day news of his death came through and announced it on the six o'clock news bulletin; I found it hard to keep the emotion out of my voice.

Before the *Today* programme moved from Broadcasting House to Television Centre at White City in west London in the late 1990s, many politicians were keen to come into the studio in person and take part in a highly entertaining form of political jousting with whichever *Today* presenter was interviewing them. I loved observing the ebb and flow of political debate, politician versus journalist, each determined to emerge triumphant from the scrap. I thought how lucky I was to watch from the sidelines, knowing I would never have to submit myself to the forensic questioning of John Humphrys, tenacious as a terrier, persistently seeking out the truth of what politicians were up to. I always enjoyed the occasions when Kenneth Clarke was a live guest. He was supremely relaxed, confident in his own ability to more than hold his own in debate and with a very cheery, friendly manner. He had an extremely quick mind but also liked to laugh, which made his appearances a winning combination of geniality and great acuity. On one occasion he was so relaxed he winked at me during the course of one of Jim Naughtie's famously long questions!

I loved working with Jim – my spirits always lifted when I got into work for the early shift and learned that he would be presenting that morning. He was always cheerful, in spite of the early hour, and I thoroughly enjoyed listening to his astute analysis of domestic and international politics, as well as his amusing stories. I also liked and admired his use of the English language and always try to listen to his excellent *Book Club* programmes on Radio 4.

Lord Carrington, who was a regular guest on the programme, was charming and urbane. He remained completely unruffled by any hostile questioning and always replied in perfectly formed, grammatically correct sentences. John Redwood, by contrast, appeared to be ill at ease to the point of shiftiness; his eyes darted about as if unsure where to settle. He was what my father would have called 'a cold fish'. Perhaps because of his undoubted cleverness he never established any empathy with the electorate. He would never be a popular politician and will always be remembered as the Secretary of State for Wales who didn't know the words of the Welsh National Anthem. He was caught on camera attempting to mouth them and looking excruciatingly uncomfortable in the process.

An entrepreneur who came on the programme failed to understand that he was meant to keep quiet while the bulletin was being read. I was in the middle of reading a cue during the eight o'clock news when he suddenly barked out, 'I don't know what to do with these headphones'. Frantic hand signals from my editor sitting beside me failed to quieten him, so that his voice and mine could be heard in an unusual duet for a short while until I thankfully reached the end of the cue. While the insert was being played he asked me if I would 'be a love' and fetch him a cup of coffee. I took great delight in telling him that I was otherwise engaged!

I lived dangerously on occasion when stepping into the *Today* studio. On New Year's Eve 2003 the atmosphere was suitably festive. The head barman from the Savoy Hotel had been invited in to mix a cocktail called a Corpse Reviver and Jim offered me a taste. It lived up to its name and was powerfully medicinal; the back of my throat suddenly ceased to exist, but that proved to be the least of my problems. The head barman was asked to continue mixing some drinks and took to his task with alacrity. I, however, was meant to be reading a news summary at the same time. It's not an easy thing to do with a silver cocktail shaker being brandished by your left ear and then shaken loudly and vigorously. The finer points of Britain's economic performance got lost amidst a general outburst of merriment and revelry!

The Great Storm of 16 October 1987 proved how well *Today* responded to big stories, rising to the challenge with great professionalism in trying circumstances. I was on an overnight shift that night and sleep had been particularly elusive for the four short hours of 'rest' we got between the end of the midnight bulletin and the start of *Today*. The powerful, unceasing winds nearly blew in the ancient sash windows of the hostel where I was staying, with each successive gust. I felt as if I was in my own private production of *Wuthering Heights* and could hear large objects being blown around until they shattered in the street below. An apocalyptic scene faced me when I walked from the hostel into Broadcasting House. Debris was strewn everywhere, a brick wall had collapsed, some trees had lost branches and I could hear the incessant beeping of car alarms. Broadcasting House was operating on an emergency generator because of a power cut in the area. Scripts had to be written by candlelight and there was very subdued lighting in the studio, making it hard to read the summaries and bulletins. There was also a nauseating smell of diesel oil in the building. In spite of these conditions I remember a particularly happy and good-natured programme that morning, the spirit of the Blitz seemingly resurrected as everybody did their best in difficult circumstances. Sue MacGregor and John Humphrys presented the programme with admirable professionalism and skill, reporting on the devastation that the storm had wrought.

I was slightly wary of meeting John Humphrys when I heard that he was going to present the *Today* programme. His reputation as an attack dog preceded him and I wondered what he would be like in person. When I walked into the studio, introduced myself and shook his hand he greeted me effusively – so much so that I thought he must have mistaken me for someone else. I was right – he later admitted that he'd thought I was someone he'd met before. He is good company, sometimes bracingly so, and is alert, quick-witted and ever ready for an argument. You can't be lulled into thinking he's a pussycat that wants its ears tickled; any remark that couldn't be substantiated was pounced upon and you had to be prepared to stand your ground and fight back. Sometimes when he did this in front of other guests it felt as if he was grandstanding a little bit, going on the attack just for the hell of it and the sheer delight of being combative.

It was often stated – jokingly – that John had more than his fair share of testosterone and on occasion he would chunter away and grumble if something or someone had bugged him. As soon as he'd read the headlines

before the main bulletin at eight o'clock he would then
be out of his chair, flinging open the heavy studio door
and starting a heated discussion and/or argument with
the programme's editor in the time it took me to read the
first three lines of the lead cue. The door would take an
age to swing shut and his animated debate would provide an urgent counterpoint to the measured pace of my
reading. Sarah Montague, who is genial and laid-back,
would take it all in her stride, roll her eyes and laugh.
He could usually be cajoled back into good humour and
Sarah was adept at this. She dealt with him beautifully,
gently teasing him and pulling his leg, usually about
his refusal to embrace fully modern technology and the
delights or otherwise of social media. Like most people
he has mellowed with age and doesn't mind being teased
– in fact he often seems to actively enjoy it. I got on well
with him and admired his professionalism; observing
him conduct an interview with clinical precision and
seeing the way the argument flowed back and forth until
he nailed the person he was questioning was like a masterclass in the art of political interviewing. I may have
concentrated too much on his Rottweiler tendencies –
he was kind to me and we often enjoyed a joke and a
laugh. I still enjoy listening to him close in on a hapless
interviewee and admire his ability to think quickly on
his feet and pounce whenever there's a flaw in his guest's
argument. I shall miss him enormously when he finally
hangs up his headphones, but I'm convinced he'll still

be broadcasting deep into his eighth decade. Public life and discourse is much the richer for his presence.

The advent of Justin Webb and Evan Davis breathed new life into the programme; they're bright, quick and have demonstrated a lovely light touch. I feel something exciting is always about to happen when they're on air and listening to them throughout the course of a three-hour programme is a refreshing and stimulating experience. I greatly enjoyed their company in the studio, and to observe them in action, co-presenting with each other or with Sarah, was always good fun.

A lot of comment and discussion has taken place about the lack of air-time on the programme given to women in comparison with men. The balance is slowly being redressed but I'm often aware that whole swathes of the *Today* programme go by without a woman's voice making a contribution to the national debate. I can think of many women whom I've met in the studio who've impressed me a great deal. They include Baroness Boothroyd, the former Speaker of the House of Commons – the first and so far only female Speaker. She was described by both Sir John Major and Tony Blair as an 'outstanding' Speaker; the word 'redoubtable' could have been coined just for her and she's a woman after my own heart in that she's a football supporter – her team is West Bromwich Albion.

It was a privilege to witness at first hand the inner workings of this broadcasting institution over the course of twenty-seven years, to observe the body language of the politicians of the day, the interplay between the interviewer and interviewee, and the jocular informality of the presenters. The latter have virtually all been a remarkably good-humoured group, considering the time of day that they broadcast. The atmosphere is usually relaxed and laid-back, jokes and banter a necessary and vital part of the equation. I particularly liked working with the pairing of Sue MacGregor and Jim Naughtie. In my opinion Sue was – and remains – the pre-eminent female radio presenter of the past forty years. Blessed with a superb broadcasting voice, she has reported and presented with distinction on *The World at One*, *Woman's Hour*, *Conversation Piece*, *Today*, *A Good Read* and *The Reunion*. Sue is charming and excellent company, with a very good sense of humour; I always looked forward to working with her and admired her interviewing style. She was never abrasive or aggressive, but employed a courteous persistence that invariably elicited more from the interviewee than they had planned to divulge. Her *Conversation Piece* programmes were masterpieces of the genre and should be played to all aspiring interviewers; they simply cannot be bettered. I can't understand why she has never received a damehood – she is an outstanding candidate.

Jim and I were incapable of working together without getting the giggles, certainly behind the scenes if not always on air. We shared a fairly ribald sense of humour and tended to find the same things funny. He was forever discovering little comic gems in the papers and reading them out to me, a fertile field being the obituary column in the *Daily Telegraph*. He once found a piece about a man who had taught most of the present Royal Family to ride. The paper splendidly described his work in this way – 'he mounted Prince Charles, Princess Anne and Prince Andrew'. Cue much hilarity and laughter, with me trying to pull myself together before reading my next summary. I was enormously relieved that I wasn't in the *Today* studio on the morning of the infamous Jeremy Hunt episode. Had it been me I would not have been able to carry on, having just sat through Jim's battling but vain attempts to keep the laughter at bay after committing his unfortunate spoonerism. He started to splutter and wheeze like the cartoon character Mutley, trying to explain away the vocal quavering by saying he had a bad cough. Rory Morrison, the newsreader who was on duty that morning, did a fine job. He told me later that he had to tighten every muscle in his body in order to get through the first cue of the eight o'clock bulletin, and was rewarded for doing so with a bottle of wine from the Controller of Radio 4, Gwyneth Williams.

In March 1997 I was ambushed by the giggles while reading an item on the main morning bulletin at eight o'clock. I believe it's essential to laugh at the absurdity of life and at onself, so inevitably, the laughter occasionally spills over into my work. On this particular

morning, Sue and Jim were presenting and I was preparing to read the final story of the bulletin. The voice
piece playing had ten seconds to run and the green light
in the studio had come on to warn me that it was coming
to an end. Suddenly the name of the head of Papua New
Guinea's armed forces, Major-General Sir Jack Tuat
(pronounced twat) resonated round the room. As I've
mentioned before, I have a very earthy sense of humour
and knew immediately that I was going to have trouble
getting through the next story, which to compound the
problem was about a sperm whale. In the few seconds
before the voice piece ended, Sue repeated sotto voce,
with a palpable sense of wonderment, 'Jack Twat'. I
caught her eye and from that moment knew I was lost.
My voice rose and dropped like an opera singer on speed,
the laughter broke free and the item about the stranded
sperm whale came to a premature end.

I was transported back to my ten-year-old self,
felled by the sudden, surprising intrusion of laughter
because my best friend had broken wind, unexpectedly
and explosively, during school prayers. Poor Jim managed to splutter the words 'Good luck to the whale',
before heroically embarking on an interview with Finlay
Spratt, the Head of the Northern Ireland Prison Officers'
Association. In the general chaos of the moment he was
inadvertently called Pratt. In the space of about forty
seconds we'd gone from Twat and Spratt to Pratt. It was
a moot point as to whether Sue, Jim or I slid under the

table first. I later learned that a good friend of mine in the newsroom, Tim, had deliberately edited the voice piece to ensure that the name Tuat appeared right at the end, thinking it would give me a little chuckle. He had certainly not envisaged the giggles that followed, nor the subsequent media reaction. I was interviewed by both *The Guardian* and Radio 4's *Feedback*, Jon Snow wrote a humorous column in celebration of my giggling and I received an enormous number of letters and emails from listeners who'd loved it. They were delighted to catch a rare glimpse of the human being behind the voice.

The second and final time that laughter engulfed me in twenty-seven years of live broadcasting on the BBC took place in March 2008, again right at the end of the eight o'clock bulletin. Jim – inevitably! – was presenting with Ed Stourton, another extremely pleasant and humorous colleague. The catalyst was an item featuring the earliest known recording of the human voice singing. I hadn't heard it before it went out on air and immediately thought the recording sounded like something from *The Goon Show* – querulous, crackly and faintly manic. It was a version of 'Au Clair de la Lune' and it could easily have been Peter Sellers singing it. We all laughed at how daft it sounded; unfortunately, it lasted only fourteen seconds and none of us had time to recover. At the last moment a short piece of copy was pushed in front of me about the death of the screenwriter Abby Mann.

Jim and Ed had both turned away at this point,

shoulders heaving, valiantly but vainly attempting to muffle their laughter. I started, stopped, apologised and started again, acutely aware that laughter was bubbling away dangerously inside me and any trigger, however small, would result in it bursting forth. It was like trying to stay on a bucking horse at a rodeo, desperately staving off the inevitable fall. Jim suddenly let out a particularly loud guffaw cum snort, which tipped me over the edge. The giggles became physically impossible to control and I had to yield to them until they'd run their course. I got to the end of the story, a modicum of self-control restored; Jim picked up and strove hard to keep the laughter at bay well into his next cue.

As I walked back to the newsroom from the studio I was anxious about the response from colleagues and listeners. I needn't have worried – my colleagues were delighted that something unusual had happened to spice up the morning, while listeners loved it and told me so in the hundreds of emails that swamped my inbox. The *Today* programme played the giggles again later in the programme, to the amused delight of those who hadn't heard it earlier. Helen Boaden, then the director of BBC News, came into the newsroom and gave me a big hug, saying that the incident had made her morning. Later that week I got a personal letter from Prince Charles, who wrote on headed notepaper from Birkhall to say that my 'impossibly infectious' giggling had made him laugh a lot and 'quite literally made my day'!

Back in the 1980s I read the news on *Today* alongside one of the programme's rare all-female presenting team, Sue MacGregor and Jenny Bond. I remember walking away once we were off air thinking how enjoyable it had been, blissfully free of grandstanding and showing off. All the interviews had gone well, each presenter had been impeccably professional and the world continued to turn on its axis. The only other time I've worked with an all-female team was twenty years later, when Carolyn Quinn and Sarah Montague shared presenting duties. It has often saddened me that these occasions were rare and intermittent, the women's team never establishing itself as a bedrock of the programme. Ceri Thomas, who edited the programme until early 2013, got into trouble by saying that women were not tough enough to cope in the sometimes hostile environment of the show. He did admit that the gender balance was not ideal, but appeared to stereotype women by suggesting they were not strong enough to cope with the demands of a challenging, uncompromising news and current affairs programme. He also said that it was inevitable that the male/female balance within organisations in the wider world would be reflected on air. The appointment of Mishal Hussein in July 2013 as an addition to the presentation team is definitely a great leap forward.

In the 1970s Jim Black, the Head of Presentation at Radio 4 for fourteen years, was resistant to the idea of women as programme presenters, newsreaders and continuity announcers. It was then comparatively rare to hear a female voice on air. He felt women were not capable of doing the job of a newsreader as well as men. Fortunately, Black lost the battle and women newsreaders began making their mark from 1974 onwards.

Chapter 11

THE NEWS QUIZ

THE LIGHTS WERE low and as usual the atmosphere was uncomfortably warm and close. The Drill Hall was a sweaty, intimate venue, with room for about 300 people. *The News Quiz* was held there when the Radio Theatre was unavailable and those of us taking part were corralled behind a thick felt curtain in near-darkness waiting to be introduced and go on stage.

The mood was good-natured and slightly anarchic, and the audience, being warmed up by our chair, Simon Hoggart, sounded warm and responsive. We all felt it was going to be a good show. Alan Coren, the wonderfully inventive lynchpin of the programme, found a child's wooden rocking-horse backstage and brought it on with him. Cue much ribaldry and laughter as Alan mounted it and the tone was set for a particularly funny evening. Sometimes if the show went through a few longueurs or it became too hot in the hall, people would leave early. The only way to exit was to clatter down the steps and past the panel. If Jeremy Hardy was on he would harangue them loudly and very funnily about their poor bladder control or lack of respect for those taking part. This routine always got a huge laugh and the poor victim would scuttle away looking mortified, unsure whether to laugh or cry. On this particular night, however, everyone stayed in their seats, completely involved in the comic chaos unfolding before them.

The panel comprised two very funny, talented women – Sandi Toksvig, who now chairs the show, and the extraordinarily gifted Linda Smith, whose comic timing was a thing of beauty – as well as Alan, and Andy Hamilton, another clever, witty and generous comic. The highlight of the night came when Sandi mentioned that it was National Condom Week and that she'd received a measuring device to help you decide which condom would fit best. Sandi, beginning to bubble with laughter, said she'd thought it was a device to measure spaghetti. Simon, naughtily and with faux innocence, asked if it measured the spaghetti before or after it was put in boiling water. Linda chose the perfect moment to ask, 'Was it *al dente*?' It was such a privilege to be working with them all that night; they were at their very best and it was a joy to witness. The memories are coloured by sadness however: Linda, Alan and Simon are no longer with us and they all died far too early.

The News Quiz is satirical, witty and sometimes gloriously smutty. Since 1977 when it was first broadcast, the panel – comprising comedians and journalists – takes a sharp, quick-witted sideswipe at current affairs and politicians. The newsreaders love taking part because the programme allows them to play the part of a court jester to the hilt, reading out comically surreal cuttings from the newspapers. I think I was deliberately given the most risqué cuttings the producer could get away with broadcasting on Radio 4, in the full knowledge that I had a very ribald sense of humour and would struggle to get through it without cracking up. On one occasion we even rehashed a story that I'd had to read on the six o'clock bulletin about a man who had accidentally shot himself in the testicles.

Not long after I'd started to be a regular newsreader on the programme I read out a cutting that elicited a huge, collective guffaw from the audience. In the sea off Bournemouth a woman on an inflatable teddy bear had had to be rescued by a man on an inflatable set of false teeth – this brought the first big laugh – and then I went on to say, 'A spokesman for the coastguard said that this sort of thing was becoming all too common', which, as they say, brought the house down.

Another favourite was this one: 'Shoplifters are becoming ever more exotic in their choice of goods. In New York, light-fingered Sybil Serth was rushed to hospital with hypothermia, after concealing six frozen quails in her bra and four more in her knickers. "My son must have put them there when I wasn't looking," she later explained.'

I've been lucky enough to have had a long and happy association with *The News Quiz*. I first appeared on the programme as the newsreader in 1986 when it was recorded at the Paris Theatre, also known as the Paris Studios, in Lower Regent Street. It used to be a cinema and was converted into a theatre by the BBC for radio broadcasts, becoming the main venue for radio programmes. It was small and intimate and ideal for radio comedy audiences. In 1995 it closed and was replaced by the newly refurbished Art Deco BBC Radio Theatre in Broadcasting House. Barry Took was the chairman at that time, having taken up the position in 1979. He was kind and avuncular and had – like all the great comics – superb comic timing. He was also a marvellous master of the pun and took gleeful delight in telling a funny story. Barry was a pioneer of radio comedy and was extremely knowledgeable on the subject. He co-wrote the very popular comedy classic *Round the Horne* with Marty Feldman, and was therefore responsible for a wealth of gloriously rude double entendres as well as popularising polari, the risqué patois of the then homosexual subculture, immortalised by Julian and Sandy, aka Kenneth Williams and Hugh Paddick.

I remember travelling up to York on the train with Barry and Alan Coren en route to a *News Quiz* outside broadcast. They were in first class and invited me to sit with them, charming the train conductor into letting me stay. It was like witnessing a masterclass in the telling of comic tales and anecdotes. I laughed so much that I became breathless and ached all over – and it wasn't just me who appreciated their double act. The rest of the carriage, previously absorbed in their work, began to listen and were soon casting admiring glances at Barry and Alan, fascinated by their performance in spite of themselves. When we were all turfed off at Doncaster because of a fault in the train's engine, a number of passengers thanked them for making the journey so enjoyable.

Alan was on a roll by now and suggested, as we waited on the platform for a replacement train, that we re-enact the speck in the eye scene from the film *Brief Encounter*. He was to be Trevor Howard, I was Celia Johnson and Barry played Stanley Holloway. Alan, who was quite a bit smaller than me, played his part with manic gusto. I perfected a cut-glass 1950s middle England accent and had to bend my knees when Alan wanted to look in my eye. Barry couldn't stop chortling at the sheer daftness of it all. Throughout this entire episode we were watched by a stolid station porter. At the end of our little enactment he said, 'Some people would pay good money to see that', then a killer pause, 'but not me.' That made Barry chortle all the more and he was still laughing when we finally made it to York.

I did a number of outside broadcasts with the *News Quiz* team, most enjoyably at the Edinburgh Festival, where we appeared at the Pleasance Theatre and had a great time. On that occasion we flew up to Scotland, but we usually got the train to other destinations in the UK. Once, on a journey to Cheltenham, we had seats booked but found to our dismay – after walking down the entire length of the train – that the carriage didn't exist. Linda launched into a very funny riff about the missing carriage and asked – with round-eyed innocence – if we were on a ghost train. She then speculated as to where the carriage actually was – had it been abandoned in a field and left to its fate? The poor conductor to whom all this was directed didn't know how to respond and eventually backed away with a wild look in his eye. Linda was so entertaining that day, the rest of us didn't mind that our seats were non-existent and we had to stand the whole way.

At another venue out of London we were invited to a civic reception after the recording. These can be a mixed blessing – it's quite fun to meet people afterwards, but the panel are usually keen to catch the last train and get home as quickly as possible. We certainly didn't want to listen to an interminable oration from the mayor and then another lengthy speech from the deputy mayor. It was also uncomfortably hot in the overcrowded room.

We began to despair of ever getting out of there, but our producer was a mistress of diplomacy and we managed to extricate ourselves. On the way home in the train we sang show tunes and Linda demonstrated her phenomenal knowledge of films and cricket.

Linda had a huge and immediate impact on *The News Quiz* when she joined the team in 1998. She was exceptionally funny and quick-witted; this, combined with her generosity of spirit, led the audience to fall in love with her, just as they had with Sandi Toksvig, Alan Coren, Jeremy Hardy and Andy Hamilton. Linda was always friendly and approachable in the Green Room before the show and would invariably come over to chat and have a laugh with me. One night, before the advent of mobile phones, she asked me what on earth I'd been up to in central London. When I looked puzzled she claimed to have found calling cards in telephone booths in the West End. They apparently showed a picture of a scantily clad woman wielding a whip with the heading 'Charlotte Green – very strict diction'. It was a wonderful joke and indicative of her fertile comic imagination. I told it to the audience in the Drill Hall when we recorded a tribute show for Linda following her very untimely death in 2006. They loved it, but that was no surprise because they loved everything about Linda. In the same show I read a piece that she had written for *The Beaton Generation* on BBC Radio 4, called 'National Pet Week'. She began by saying, 'I realised it was about animal awareness

– anyone who uses pavements for walking on can't help but be aware of them! Make the dogshit slalom an Olympic sport and there's your British gold medal.' Vintage Linda.

Corrie Corfield and I went to the Purcell Room on the South Bank to read out some more of Linda's hilarious musings, as part of another tribute show that her lovely partner Warren Lakin had organised. Standing in the wings waiting to go on, Corrie and I were a little apprehensive because we wanted to do it well for Linda's sake. We also felt proud and honoured that Warren had asked us to take part. Later in the year, the two of us joined Peter Donaldson and Brian Perkins in a wonderful evening at the Victoria Palace Theatre, London. It was a tribute gig called 'Tippy Top: An Evening of Linda's Favourite Things'. Peter, Brian, Corrie and I got to 'sing' – in a kind of Rex Harrison way – with the Blockheads, one of Linda's favourite bands, at the end of the show. It was an incredibly visceral experience, combining great excitement with the sheer power of the music to wonderful effect. The sobriety and restrained gravitas of a news bulletin and studio seemed such a remote world at that point. The four of us couldn't stop laughing afterwards, the energy and emotion fizzing and bubbling out of us. But we never forgot why we were there – the love and affection for Linda was so palpable that night.

It seems extraordinary, thinking back now to the 1990s, that even when I was invariably the only woman on the stage for a *News Quiz* recording, that was acceptable because I was in a subsidiary position reading out the funny cuttings. Sandi and Linda, two of the funniest women in the country, very rarely appeared on the programme together. The producers didn't seem to like having two women on the panel. Of course, when Linda and Sandi *did* appear on the show together, they were highly successful. Astonishingly, Linda was taken off *The News Quiz* for a while because Radio 4 wanted to try out other women. Why on earth should a woman replace another woman; what was wrong with having two women and two men?

Fortunately, Linda soon became an established part of the *News Quiz* team, as did other talented comics and comedy performers such as Susan Calman, Rebecca Front and Bridget Christie. Sandi took over as chair from Simon Hoggart in 2006 and her speed of thought, wittiness and comic timing immediately shone through to great effect. I enjoyed working with all three chairs – Barry, Simon and Sandi. Simon was a little shy, kind and welcoming. He wore large glasses, which gave him an owlish look, and had a ready smile. I always enjoyed my read-throughs with him before the others turned up. He was steeped in the world of politics and invariably had something acute to say about politicians and policy. His knowledge of wine was vast and he gave me some very good advice about what bottles to buy! He died from cancer early in 2014 and I'm very sad that I won't see his smile again or be entertained by his excellent anecdotes.

Sandi is wonderful company and the perfect Chair: warm, welcoming and generous. She always made me feel completely at home and one of the *News Quiz* family, which I greatly appreciated. We always seemed to end up convulsed with laughter whenever we did our read-throughs and sound-checks together. She seemed to know everything about all sorts of arcane subjects and I came away from each *News Quiz* session knowing a little bit more about the world. Sandi is now Chancellor of Portsmouth University – in my opinion an inspired appointment, such is her love of learning and knowledge. I once unwittingly made her burst into laughter while she showed me round the site of a house she was having rebuilt. We were scrambling round the scaffolding and I turned and told her to mind her head. Sandi, who is famously small – barely five feet – managed to gasp through gusts of laughter that NO ONE had ever before had reason to warn her to mind her head!

Another big favourite of mine is Jeremy Hardy, who has been appearing on the show for many years and is now a much-loved stalwart. *The News Quiz* wouldn't feel right without Jeremy's gloriously rude rants. He's an intelligent, thoughtful man who was very kind to me when first my father, and then a few years later, my mother died. It was done unobtrusively and meant a great deal to me. When he first joined the show he used to jokingly play the role of a creepy 'uncle', circa the 1950s, in the Green Room before the recording. He'd put on a fruity Terry Thomas voice and introduce me as his niece whom he'd put up in a flat in central London. Occasionally he did this during the recording and got a big laugh. Often after I'd read out a particularly rude or smutty cutting, chosen especially for me in the hope that I would corpse, he would immediately denounce me as a 'filthy cow'. It always got a warm response from the audience. On the way back from an outside broadcast in Cheltenham we all had to pile into a cramped mini-van. It was physically very uncomfortable as there were far too many of us trying to fit in. Jeremy, however, kept up a brilliantly funny – and rude – monologue for virtually the whole journey, which made it much more bearable.

The News Quiz was being recorded the night of my farewell party, but the whole team came and had some drinks with me before they started, which was a nice gesture. Afterwards, Jeremy joined me and my friends and family for a late meal at an Italian trattoria round the back of Broadcasting House. I've still got the farewell presents he gave me – one of them a set of notecards with tiny figures set in a vast landscape. If you look closely the little people are doing very rude things! The other gift was a pair of hand-warmers in the shape of skimpy Y-fronts that fit handily in the pocket. As the packaging said: 'The only knickers that you can put in your pocket without feeling like it's the walk of shame.' Classic Jeremy!

Chapter 12

CLOSE ENCOUNTERS WITH THE RADIO 4 AUDIENCE

AUDIENCES CAN BE fickle and I've often wondered, while taking part in *The News Quiz*, why an audience can be so warm and responsive one week and so sticky and stolid the next. When I first started on the show there used to be a man who came in every week, but who seemed determined not to laugh at anything that was said. People would be rocking with laughter all round him but he would remain steadfastly morose and unsmiling. It gave him a faint air of madness and it was certainly unsettling to see him sitting there, utterly mirthless, after I'd just read out a supposedly funny cutting. If the show was taking place at the Drill Hall rather than the Radio Theatre, I had to walk through people milling round the entrance or having a drink with friends before coming into the recording. This was usually fine and some of the crowd would say hello and wish me all the best. There was one young bloke, however, who I did my best to avoid. His modus operandi was to stand right in front of me and greet me effusively; I think he was harmless, but the gushing approach was off-putting. I used to smile, say hello and then sidestep him — I didn't want to get enmeshed in further conversation. As I passed, he would turn to whoever he was with and say very loudly, 'That's Charlotte Green — she's a close personal friend of mine.' It always made me laugh as I barely knew him and it became a running gag with my friends. Whenever someone famous came up in conversation we would all laugh and claim that he or she was a close personal friend, or CPF for short.

I've just recently recorded a series of *Quote...Unquote* at the Radio Theatre, reading out the quotations. One evening a man was sitting in the front row with his gorgeous guide dog, a cream Labrador. With exquisite timing, about four minutes into the recording, the dog stood up, yawned and shook itself and then started to scratch itself very loudly. It was very funny and almost seemed deliberate. The noise was quite intrusive, so we had to re-record a short section at the end of the session. Just before we did so, someone asked what the dog was called – 'Acorn' replied her owner, at which point the dog shot up, shook itself loudly again and waited patiently to have its harness put on, thinking it was back on duty. The audience loved it and Acorn became the star of the show.

Early on in my career at the BBC the producer of *In Touch* asked if I would meet a boy of about ten, who was completely blind and who enjoyed listening to me on the radio. He was a lovely, lively child who regarded his blindness as an inconvenience rather than a handicap, and just got on with his life. He asked if he could feel my face and hair as that was his way of working out what I looked like. The radio played an important part in his daily life and he was extremely well informed about Radio 4. He made a lasting impression on me because of his openness, evident relish for life and curiosity about the world. I'm sure I got far more out of the meeting than he did.

I like the way children are excited about things that adults barely notice or take for granted. A friend's little boy used to stand right in front of the radio whenever she told him that I was on, and believed for a while that I lived inside the set – an echo of my sister's belief that I thought there were little creatures hidden inside the radio, who were responsible for the sounds emanating from it. On the day that I got the giggles on the *Today* programme, my friend's little boy was upset because he thought that my 'teacher' would probably tell me off. To cheer me up he drew me a large picture of a spider doing a poo – bodily functions seem to exert a fascination over all children, not least me when I was the same age! Years ago the small daughter of another friend asked me very seriously if flies had bottoms – I replied that they probably did, at which point she asked if they did poos. I got drawn into a rather tricky debate that went on for a few minutes. Eventually, she looked at me gravely and said that she didn't think that I really knew the answer. Suitably chastened, I suggested that we went on a butterfly hunt in the garden and she readily agreed, all thoughts of insects' bottoms thankfully banished. I was exactly the same when I was a child, forever asking questions with a scatological bias.

Back in the '80s an exhibition on all things radio was held at Earl's Court. The announcers took turns spending a day there and handing out publicity photos, chatting to the public and reading news summaries from inside a glass box, specially designed to allow people to watch us as we broadcast. In theory this was a good idea, but the reality proved otherwise. It was very distracting having people milling around on all sides of the little ad hoc studio. It's really not very easy trying to concentrate on the summary – going live into Radio 4 – when you can see someone picking their nose out of the corner of your eye.

Throughout the day I had noticed an elderly woman

standing quietly to one side, staring intently into the cubicle. After one broadcast I invited her in and asked her if she was enjoying her visit. She said she was, and then blurted out that she was fascinated by my feet they were very small for someone of my height! I'm not often lost for words, but I couldn't think what to say in response. Eventually I laughed and said that a size five wasn't too small for a woman of 5ft 9in. She laughed as well and said she thought that my feet looked very neat, after which she got up and left. It was an instructive lesson – I'd fondly imagined that she would be interested in the news broadcasts, but instead her rapt attention was the result of her fascination with my feet.

A journalist in the newsroom once remarked that he couldn't understand why I didn't topple over, so small were my plates of meat. Fortunately, I rarely fall over, but on one spectacular occasion I got my feet caught up in the long, looped lead of my headphones and went down like a steer caught in a lasso. I'd just finished reading the midnight news and was looking forward to going home and getting into bed. Instead I spent the whole night in the A&E department of the local hospital, accompanied by a very kind newsroom colleague. As I fell I hit a large, sharp-edged, old-fashioned tape-machine, which had been left in the studio, and as a result ended up with a broken rib, two deep cuts on my leg and spectacular bruising. The day before my sister had broken a bone in her ankle while walking in the Peak District, so when we got together we looked like a couple of extras from *Holby City*. I really enjoy sharing laughter with friends, but the hardest part of my recuperation was trying not to laugh, because of the extreme pain in my ribs when I did so.

In 2002 while I was off sick with glandular fever, the *Radio Times* ran a competition to find the nation's favourite male and female voices on the radio. I was vaguely aware that I'd been nominated and that *Radio Times* readers were being invited to vote, but was feeling so listless that I didn't really take much notice. Some days I barely had enough energy to lift a toothbrush and clean my teeth. Weeks passed, and still I felt utterly lethargic and lacking in energy. A phone call from work, however, cheered me up considerably, when I learned that I had won the competition, alongside Terry Wogan, who'd won the favourite male voice category. I got off the phone and exhausted myself by trying to make a celebratory cup of tea.

It was decided that when I'd recovered sufficiently I would go into Broadcasting House for a photoshoot with Terry Wogan; the resulting photo would then be on the front cover of the *Radio Times*, with another photo and short article inside. The day of the shoot was long and exhausting; I still wasn't fully fit and hadn't regained my usual energy. Despite this I found the whole experience fascinating and definitely developed a taste for being pampered! A make-up artist turned up at my house early in the morning and worked on my face and hair for an hour until a car came to take us into the BBC. He made me up beautifully, using very subtle colours and shades, which highlighted my brown eyes. It was like watching a painter at work, with my face as his canvas and a palette of paints replaced by myriad shades of eye shadow. As he worked he told me how, as a small boy growing up in South Africa, he would watch his mother applying her make-up and was intrigued by the process by which she transformed her face. His other great love was three-day eventing – he owned horses and I think he said he was good enough to compete at Badminton. By the end of the session I was even commiserating with him over having been dumped by his boyfriend via text message, which must have been deeply wounding. He'd also – hilariously – let me in on some of the tricks of the trade employed on the more mature woman to combat the inexorable pull of gravity. Apparently the subtle application of Sellotape behind the ears works wonders. One day maybe I'll resort to a judicious use of Magic tape to kid myself that I look rejuvenated, although having done years of early starts and late finishes I may need industrial-strength gaffer tape to counteract the sagging.

The photoshoot was fun, in spite of the fact that Terry and I spent a considerable amount of time turning this way and that, grinning, smiling winsomely, or sometimes inadvertently gurning! After a while the muscles around my mouth began to tire and I felt sure I was developing an unappealing rictus grin. In the end the photo chosen for the front cover was lovely, as was the picture on the inside pages – a real tribute to the skill and patience of the photographer. It's a head and shoulders shot of the two of us side by side smiling at the camera, with a silver microphone positioned between us at the exact centre of the picture. The caption reads 'Look who's talking. The radio voices that turn you on.' When the *Radio Times* came out I went to my local supermarket and – showing remarkable restraint – restricted myself to buying just three copies! I still have them and they're in pristine condition. I've rooted one of them out to prompt my memory of the occasion – I see a younger version of myself looking out from the cover, but also a remarkably well-groomed version. The make-up artist did a marvellous job and it's lovely to have a reminder that once upon a time I scrubbed up really rather well! A few months later I was sent a large, framed picture of the *Radio Times* front cover, which now hangs on a wall unobtrusively on the landing.

I was also very flattered to be awarded the Roberts Radio Special Award for Excellence in Broadcasting in 2009. The awards ceremony was organised by the Voice of the Listener and Viewer and took place at the Geological Society in Burlington House, Piccadilly. I received a limited edition digital Roberts radio – a very welcome addition to my burgeoning collection of radios!

I've often wondered why it was that listeners frequently asked for photographs, signed or otherwise.

Nowadays the internet can provide any number of images, but in pre-digital days it must have been a desire to possess something physical that could be held or placed on a mantelpiece. Curiosity is often the spur, a desire to put a face to the voice and to judge how closely reality matches imagination. The greeting I invariably receive when being introduced to people I haven't met before is 'it's so nice to put a face to the voice'. On the flip side I was bored to conniptions by the number of people who came up to the Radio 4 desk at the Earl's Court exhibition, surveyed the publicity photos and said, 'Oh, you've all got great faces for radio.' Without exception they all thought that what they were saying was astoundingly witty and fresh-minted. My inner voice was shouting, 'Speak for yourself, mate' or 'Have you looked in the mirror lately?', but I would smile beatifically and ask them an anodyne question about their favourite programmes. The conversations with people who were genuinely enthusiastic about the network, however, were always enjoyable.

I once received what I initially thought was a polite request for a publicity photograph. From innocuous beginnings, however, it rapidly descended into an enquiry into my bra size and whether I had a photo showing me in a wet T-shirt. Judging from the somewhat spidery writing and the address at the top of the letter – a residential home for the elderly – this was clearly a man determined to rage against the dying of the light.

At a BBC radio show in Nottingham in the late 1980s I

was expected to act as an ambassador for Radio 4, extolling the many and varied delights of the network. Along with my colleagues from other stations, I was also asked to hand out publicity photos and car stickers. My diplomatic skills were sorely tested when a girl of about nine swept most of the photos off the desk and into a plastic bag in one swift, well-practised movement. When I suggested she might like to put some of them back, she yelled 'Eff off' and darted away, no doubt to launch a similar raid on the Radio 2 desk. Amazingly she returned later and asked me to sign some of the photos. My anarchic side asserted itself. I couldn't resist signing one as Brian Perkins, another as Victoria Station and a third, childishly but with particular relish, as Hugh Jarse. She didn't bat an eyelid.

One of the great delights of working in radio is the relative anonymity it affords me. I can walk down the street to my local shops, dressed very casually, and no one will stare, thinking that they've seen me on television but can't quite remember in what programme. I'm a private person doing a public job, but the freedom to walk unrecognised through public spaces suits me very well. That is, until I open my mouth and speak.

I went to a jewellers one afternoon to get my watch repaired. I explained what I wanted done and gave the shop-owner my watch; he took it, looked at me and said, 'You're Charlotte Green, aren't you?' I must have looked astounded – he smiled and explained that he listened to

Radio 4 all day long while doing his repairs and knew most of the regular voices well. Hence the educated guess. We chatted for a long time about the BBC – he was a keen and committed listener who loved the diversity of the programmes and the sheer breadth of subjects covered.

While on holiday in Cornwall, some friends and I had stopped for a cream tea in a tiny, remote village after a long coastal walk. I went into the tea shop and ordered for everyone and then walked outside to join my friends at a table in the sun. I'd been dimly aware that a cyclist had parked his bike and come into the shop behind me. As he passed my table he smiled and said, 'Hello Charlotte, I'd know your voice anywhere.' I laughed and congratulated him on guessing who I was. He'd been an actor and was now teaching in Cornwall; he explained that he was very attuned to voices. His wife came up to join us and we all had a friendly conversation about Cornwall and its beautiful coastline. When they finished their tea, they popped back into the tea shop, which doubled as a gift shop – and bought me a present of a little box with a painting of a Cornish chough on the lid. It was a lovely, thoughtful gesture and I often think of that chance meeting that took place on a perfect summer's afternoon. There have been other occasions when my voice has been recognised and each time the people concerned have been charming and friendly. I'm not sure how I would react if someone were to be rude or antagonistic; probably

I'd shrug my shoulders and walk away. I loathe any form of aggressive confrontation. Fortunately, it has never happened and I hope it never will. Meanwhile I happily walk around my neighbourhood unremarked and unnoticed, and that's just how I like it.

Radio exerts a kind of magic over its listeners because they have to use their imagination to conjure up visual images prompted by the voice. Intriguingly, people have always thought that I sounded as if I was tall, which I am. More often than not they're surprised to discover I'm fair-haired rather than dark. That's what I love about the medium of radio – it allows you to give your imagination free rein and provide your own pictures. Discovering how close your own images are to the actual face behind the voice is all part of the fun.

Chapter 13

CHARLOTTE – THE FISHERMAN'S FRIEND

FROM THE TIME I started reading the Shipping Forecast in 1985 I built up a loyal following. People have always associated me with this haunting, five-minute incantatory recitation of sea areas along the entire coast of the UK. It is the nearest I ever came to reading poetry on air; the place names had their own special beauty and the forecast its own internal rhythms and cadences. Whenever I read it I was always struck by its unique, haunting beauty as well as the more mundane reality of reading it to time and not crashing the pips! When I was in continuity the tyranny of the pips loomed large; it was a matter of professional pride never to kiss them, crash them or ride roughshod through the whole lot.

It seemed that the Radio 4 audience liked the way I read the Shipping Forecast – I always aimed to read it clearly and distinctly and at a measured pace to enable sailors on fishing boats, wallowing in deep angry seas, to write it down. It was one of the subjects I received the most letters about and whenever people meet me they invariably ask me to 'say a few lines' from it. Bizarrely, some people still think I read it out on air now, even though I stopped reading it when I concentrated solely on newsreading. One letter-writer accused me of saying *shitting* forecast and threatened to write to the Controller of Radio 4 in disgust at my use of bad language. Predictably the letter was written in green ink! People often gave me handkerchiefs, mugs and tea-towels printed with a map of the UK and the Shipping Forecast areas. I used to quite like receiving these, but after the first thirty or so they rather lost their appeal. The late Simon Hoggart, whom I greatly enjoyed working with on *The News Quiz*, wrote in *The Guardian* in 2005, when I started reading the late Shipping Forecast again, that I was 'Charlotte, the fisherman's friend', and the name stuck. Writing in the same paper in 2009, the author Adam Nicolson wrote memorably of sailors caught in a terrifying storm, listening to the simple words of the Shipping Forecast and existing in 'a sodden, fragile environment, the fear of the big sea breaking behind you, the unspeakable longing for harbours and quiet'. He wonderfully captures the essence of the Shipping Forecast's poetry – 'vastness and violence described in tranquillity'.

The journalist Oliver Pratchett wrote a very funny spoof Shipping Forecast in 2002, on learning that the name Finisterre was being dropped in the forecast in favour of Fitzroy. 'Cromarty, a faithful aged manservant, working for the crusty General Synopsis, had served him in the bloody civil war which led to South Utsire breaking away from North Utsire. Sadly he'd had both his Hebrides shot off, just below the Faeroes.' It went on in similar vein, cleverly working in all the sea area names.

Early in 1997, I was invited by Julian May, a producer on *Kaleidoscope*, Radio 4's arts programme, to review an exhibition of black and white photographs by Mark Power called The Shipping Forecast. Mark had travelled to all thirty-one sea areas and captured the essence of each place, cleverly challenging our assumptions about them. He is a leading documentary photographer and so the work was intense and powerful, occasionally provocative. I met him in Brighton, where the exhibition was held, and was intrigued to learn how the Shipping Forecast had captured his imagination. There were two photographs that particularly held my attention. Cromarty, with the caption 'Westerly veering Northwesterly, 4 or 5, occasionally 6, showers, good', shows a scruffy beach with the tide going out, leaving stray bundles of seaweed on the shoreline. Overhead the clouds are dark, lowering and oppressive. On the beach a boy of about five, oblivious to everything around him, makes abstract patterns in the sand with what looks like an enormous quill pen. What really draws the eye, however, is a vast oil rig hogging the horizon. It's a quirky yet beautiful image and I kept returning to it as I walked round the exhibition.

My other favourite image was the photograph of Rockall, which confirmed rather than confounded my expectation. It is as bleak, remote and harsh as I had imagined, a large black rock semi-submerged by a white, angry boiling sea. The spume is so all-encompassing that it resembles recently set, rough concrete. There is no sign of any sea birds alighting on the rocks or flying overhead, just a perennially churning sea and dark rock jutting out like rotting teeth. The caption was 'Westerly 7 to severe gale 9, occasionally storm 10, veering northwesterly. Showers. Moderate or good.'

A few weeks after I'd done the review for *Kaleidoscope*, Julian sent me a package with an enclosed note. It contained a copy of Mark Power's book, *The Shipping Forecast*, which he'd very kindly sent to me. Julian's note thanked me and then said, 'Look inside at the beginning.' Mark had signed the book and written 'To Charlotte for the inspiration'! I was very touched – seventeen years later the book still sits on my bookshelves.

Sitting next to it is *Rain Later, Good: Illustrating the Shipping Forecast* by the watercolour artist Peter Collyer. In 1998 we met at Broadcasting House and he told me about his project and subsequent book. He kindly told me that I had inspired him to begin his travels – 16,000 miles covered, thirty-one sea areas and thirteen coastal stations visited, two years' solid work as each painting took a minimum of one week to do. The paintings are evocative and luminous and sometimes have an ethereal quality about them. Each picture is accompanied by descriptions of Peter's thoughts and feelings on encountering each sea area. These are entertaining and individualistic, providing a sparky counterpoint to the hauntingly beautiful paintings.

I was asked to take the portrait of Peter for the inside back flap of the jacket; I even get a credit! I'm quite pleased with how the photograph turned out; Peter is standing on the steps of All Souls, Langham Place, behind him the Art Deco splendour of Broadcasting House and Eric Gill's magnificent sculpture of Prospero and Ariel.

Like Mark Power, Peter was kind enough to sign my copy of his book alongside the words 'To Charlotte, my inspiration for this work.' On the last page of the book there is a fine drawing of a puffin with a paintbrush in its mouth, standing next to a radio. I'm delighted to say that I'm the proud owner of the original drawing, given to me as a present by Peter. On a separate occasion I was asked by the producer of the film *Storm*, which starred James Nesbitt as a lighthouse-keeper, to read the Shipping Forecast for the film's soundtrack.

I've already mentioned Oliver Pratchett's spoof Shipping Forecast and there have been a number of others over the years; the format seems ideally suited to parody and satire. Roger Sawyer, a producer and editor on Radio's 4 *Broadcasting House* programme, wrote a very clever traffic forecast, referring to the clogged and congested roads of Britain as well as the myriad frustrations of drivers attempting to move around the country. He asked me to read it out on the programme and it got a huge response from listeners, all of whom identified with the depiction of thwarted attempts to drive anywhere on a clear, uncongested road.

The producers of the same programme also once asked me to read out a Shipping Forecast in Arabic, in tribute to Al Jazeera's new English-language network that launched in 2006. An Arabic-speaking journalist translated it from the English and gave me a brief lesson on how to make the correct sounds. She complimented me on having a good ear, which enabled me to pick up the words quickly. The response from the audience was fascinating – some listeners were intrigued and wanted it played again, while others were alarmed and said they didn't want the experiment repeated.

I wrote a spoof myself for the occasion of the

christening and first birthday of a friend's baby boy. I
read it out at the christening lunch.

The Shipping Forecast for Hugo

And now the Shipping Forecast for Hugo, issued at 2059
hours on Friday, 3 February 2013.

There'll be gale warnings due south, in Hugo's nether
regions, for the next forty-eight hours. Windy bottom
likely, rising to Gale Force 8 after latest feed. Less than
fragrant smell 1,000 metres, Better Out Than In.

Viking, North Utsire, South Utsire

Big smiles, happy gurgling, occasional botty pops. Wee
Wee likely, outlook fair. Nappy Rash non-existent.

Forties, Cromarty, Forth

Westerly, backing south-westerly, 3 or 4. Hugo laughing. Happily playing. Good.

Rockall, Malin, Hebrides

Southerly 4, backing south-easterly, then increasing 6
to Gale 8, perhaps 9. There'll be very high winds due
south, off the scale, eruptions – volcanic. The outlook

– two exhausted parents, eventual calm.

The outlook for Hugo

Complete and utter happiness, very contented snuffles,
bliss 200 metres, deep love – never ending.

And that completes the Shipping Forecast for Hugo.

Brian Perkins and I once wrote a joint letter to *The Times*
about the Shipping Forecast and were delighted to see
it published. An article had appeared in the paper a few
days earlier speculating about the unseen and unsung
voices that read the Shipping Forecast and mentioning
Peter Donaldson, Brian and me. Here's our reply:

Weather wise

From Mr Brian Perkins and Ms Charlotte Green

Sir, We were intrigued by Alan Hamilton's atmospheric charting of the weather and shipping forecasts
(26 August). With regard to his observation – 'We never
get to know whether Radio 4 announcers wear loud
checked jackets, sport moustaches or flash manic grins' –
here's the general synopsis of our meteorological habits.

Brian Perkins, known to his friends as Portland Bill,
disdains the donning of jackets, checked, flying or dinner.
Charlotte Green, the clean-shaven belle of Benbecula,

admits to a penchant for oilskins and sou'westers.

As to manic grins: moderate with chuckles, rising hysterically. Frequent hurricane-force screams of laughter.

Yours, drifting slowly northwards,

BRIAN PERKINS
CHARLOTTE GREEN
BBC
1 September

As I sit here writing, a new and funny spoof has emerged on the internet. It was written in response to a UKIP councillor who, upholding the party's reputation for being the natural home of eccentric, extreme-minded individuals, had claimed that the heavy rain and floods affecting the country in the winter of 2013/14 were God's response to the introduction of gay marriage. The spoof forecast has such wonderful lines as 'There are warnings of Gays in Viking, Forties, Cromarty, south-east Iceland and Bongo Bongo Land' and 'homophobic outburst, backpedalling westerly and becoming untenable'.

My favourite time for reading the Shipping Forecast was late at night, right at the end of the shift. I turned off most of the lights in the studio and had just one spotlight focused on the script. It felt intimate and private and I allowed my imagination to roam free. If the gale warnings were severe I had an image in my mind of small, relatively frail trawlers being tossed about on vast indifferent waves in the pitch-black, icy cold of a winter's night. I would imagine fishermen, clothes and hair stiff with salt, hauling themselves up a steeply angled deck with the skin of their hands and faces flayed by a biting, unforgiving wind. An evocative image of 'those in peril on the sea'. The reality was probably much more prosaic, but I've always had a romantic view of the sea – as well as being aware of its potential dangers – and grew up learning of Britain's history of naval heroes and great sea battles.

A great many people listen to the Shipping Forecast and take pleasure in it despite having no connection with the sea whatsoever. They simply love listening to the rhythmic poetry and musicality of the forecast, revelling in the place names and phrases such as 'precipitation within sight'. As I mentioned before, those listening late at night are often living on their own and lonely. For them the radio is a lifeline, the only human voice they will hear throughout the day and evening. After the late-night ships I took particular care to sign off with a very personal message, wishing listeners a safe and peaceful night. Those words at the end of my late shift brought in more letters than almost anything else I did, apart from *The News Quiz*. I realised that there was a great yearning for communication and the sound of a human voice, and that the late-night Shipping Forecast and sign-off played an important role in establishing a crucial link between the announcer and the audience.

I would receive Valentine's Day cards from sailors, although they weren't necessarily romantic in intention. A surprising number contained the pithy but distinctly unsentimental words 'Would you like to suck on a fisherman's friend?' It wasn't just cards that I received in the post – flowers and chocolates were always welcome, a sheaf of A4 pages covered in mathematical formulae less so. There was no covering note so I had no idea who had sent them or why. Brian Perkins also received similar gems in the post and we used to joke about what the calculations meant and whether Professor Stephen Hawking had sent them.

Another colleague received a cricket ball from an admirer, bizarrely covered in white paint. When she sent it back with a very polite note saying she didn't really have any need for it, she received a very dusty response. I frequently got sent biblical tracts with many an exhortation to repent of my sins. On one occasion the religious verses were accompanied by a pamphlet encouraging the reader to eat more roughage and pass softer motions!

I live in London far away from the sea, but feel a strong urge to return to the coast as often as I can. Something deep within me needs to be near water, watching the ebb and flow of the tide. I love the sight and sound of huge pounding waves and can happily sit for hours on the rocks, watching as they endlessly build before crashing in an exciting explosion of frothing foam on the beach. I think this instinctive response to the sea is why I felt such an affinity with The Shipping Forecast and loved to read out its stirring maritime poetry.

Chapter 14

MY GERMAN HOSPITAL ADVENTURE

IN LATE SEPTEMBER 2004 I went on a walking holiday to Germany and expected to be away from work for two weeks. In the event I was absent for two months, having succumbed to appendicitis halfway through the holiday. I'd spent a wonderful day walking in the hills surrounding the Rhine, the autumnal colours looking particularly stunning in the sunshine. I felt fit and happy and ate a hearty meal that evening. In the early hours of the morning I was very sick and the vomiting continued for three days, in spite of the fact that I'd stopped eating, in the mistaken belief that it was food poisoning. I was reluctant to visit a doctor and certainly didn't want to go to hospital. The sickness persisted, however, along with a certain amount of stomach pain, although this was still manageable. It was when I started to shiver uncontrollably that my sister, fluent in German, wisely decided to take me straight to an emergency doctor. He examined me and I was taken to hospital immediately.

My sister had lived in Germany for six years and worked at the British embassy in Bonn and then Berlin. Her German was excellent and so she became a vital conduit between me, the doctors and the nursing staff. Being in hospital in a foreign country, feeling really unwell and unable to communicate properly, is very isolating and lonely. Rachel would write out a list of useful phrases, such as 'I feel pain here' or 'I feel sick' and leave it with me overnight, so that I could point to it when necessary. I barely slept for the duration of the seven-day stay, worried about my inability to communicate. It didn't help that the night-nurse had all the sensitivity of a wounded bear and refused to accept that I couldn't understand what she was saying. She would stand at the end of my bed and bark something at me; when I shrugged my shoulders and pointed at the appropriate phrase on my list, she delighted in throwing her hands up in despair and giving an extravagant toss of her head. In my despair I sought sanctuary in stereotype and referred to her as the Concentration Camp Guard when talking to my sister.

My stay in a three-bed ward did not get off to an auspicious start. I was regarded as an exotic specimen by the two elderly women already in there, when they learned I was English and couldn't talk to them. My 'Get by in German' course only equipped me to order a meal or book a hotel room, rather than enquire about their knee and hip operations. I was given a pill by one of the nurses and a rather unpleasant enema. About twenty minutes later the shit almost literally hit the fan as I struggled to get to the loo. The result was catastrophic and the pristine floor was liberally spattered with the contents of my gut. The two Hausfraus looked on in horror, fascinated yet repelled at the same time. They debated this spectacular floor show long after I was tucked up in clean sheets, feeling rotten and burning inside with mortification.

The next morning I was given a suppository, much to my horror, as I'd suffered more than enough embarrassment the night before. Worse was to come. I was taken to have an X-ray of my intestines and initially all went well. The radiographer informed me that 'my diverticulates were inflammated' and sucked her teeth in an alarming manner. As the procedure drew to a close my innards let me down again; the loss of control ruined the gleaming Siemens equipment. It felt like a desecration. I kept saying 'I'm so sorry', in that very British way, while she threw her hands up in the air and exclaimed '*Mein Gott*' over and over again. It was like the Teutonic version of a Carry On film.

Fortunately my sister was there and helped clean me up and get me into a wheelchair. I still had a lot of stomach pain and could only walk doubled up. That's when the second wave of the unstoppable urge to purge began. Rachel told me to hold tight and proceeded to push me through the A&E department at great speed, scattering various hapless souls who happened to be in the way. It was a scene worthy of the Keystone Cops. We more or less made it to the nearest loo in time.

I was prepped in readiness for an operation to remove my troublesome appendix that afternoon. By then I was tired of the pain and the scatological shenanigans and was glad that soon the problem would be fixed. Rachel came down with me from the ward to the door of the operating theatre, wished me all the best and squeezed my hand. My trolley was wheeled through the double doors into a room full of light, emanating from the huge overhead arc lights. Four people dressed in surgical gowns and hats leant over and introduced themselves. The anaesthetist spoke English and explained what he was about to do; the last words I remember him saying before I became unconscious were, bizarrely, 'I love your English cookies.'

When I came round after the operation I was immediately euphoric, delighted that I was still alive and that my appendix had gone. A doctor with a kind face leant over me and asked me to evaluate the pain on a scale from one to ten. I answered six and was presumably given a shot of morphine, as my euphoria increased. I lay back feeling somewhat dopey, only dimly aware at this stage of the soreness in my side. After a period of time I was wheeled back to the ward and I drifted in and out of sleep. For some reason I suddenly snapped back into consciousness and felt thirsty. My bed was by the window and I looked out on a timeless scene – men and women working on the steeply sloping vineyards that produced the superb Riesling wines. I longed to be out there with them, fully fit and free, rather than stuck inside and subject to the constraints of hospital life.

The days passed excruciatingly slowly and the nights even more so. Rachel came in every day and her visits made my enforced stay bearable; she was also able to talk to the doctors and pass on their assessment of my progress. Every now and then a doctor would come in and examine the wound; it was kept beautifully clean and the large sterile dressing covering it was changed twice a day. A stethoscope was placed on my 'diverticulates' – as my intestines were called – daily, and one day the doctor's face lit up and she declared, 'Ah, vee heff movement!' Apparently the gut can sometimes stop working after invasive surgery, but mine was happily gurgling away. At night I was given an injection in my thigh to counteract the risk of deep vein thrombosis. I was immensely cheered one morning by the arrival of a beautiful bouquet of flowers from my good friend Jules. The colour scheme was predominantly yellow and orange and echoed the vibrant colours of the trees and vineyards outside the window.

By now I was beginning to feel very hungry, having not eaten anything for almost a week; it was a sure sign that I was recovering well. I was denied food, however, until a dietician had been to see me and so was restricted to mugs of chamomile or peppermint tea. Under normal circumstances I loathe chamomile tea, but such was the level of my deprivation that I drank it all and even asked for more. While I was savouring one such mug, a tall, attractive woman came and sat by my bed. She had an excellent bedside manner and a warm smile; in slightly stilted English she explained that she had performed the operation on me and that it was her first appendectomy! I remember thinking how glad I was that I hadn't known that before the operation. I thanked her for her skill and said I felt very well indeed, albeit hungry. She laughed, seemed delighted, shook my hand and wished me all the best. The scar, as it started to heal, was a thing of beauty: small, neat and beautifully under-stitched. It is barely noticeable because the under-stitching makes it unobtrusive. When I went to have the stitches taken out back in London, the nurse said it was the most beautiful scar she had ever seen!

I was eventually allowed a thin, very salty soup to go with my tea and it tasted like the nectar of the Gods.

This was virtually all I was allowed until I left hospital. I felt permanently hungry, but the strict diet meant that I weighed a mere 8½ stone, which coupled with my height made me look pleasingly willowy! At this point I was joined in the small ward by a woman in her early thirties, who looked troubled and frightened. It was just the two of us so we communicated with the help of a German–English pocket dictionary and the limited knowledge we possessed of each other's native tongue. She never lost her haunted look and she was thin to the point of anorexia. The dietician was forever devising nutritious meals for her to eat, but she seemed unwilling to cooperate. Her troubles seemed psychological rather than physical. At times she tried to express what she was feeling, but couldn't traverse the chasm in understanding that lay between us; the look of ineffable sadness on her face still haunts me occasionally and I hope that eventually she conquered her inner demons.

The day the doctors said I could leave hospital felt like a sudden, overwhelming release from a form of imprisonment. I was free to join the real world again, free to be an independent person and above all free from the constraints of illness. I felt blessed and very fortunate. The long drive back through Germany, Belgium and France was a bit of an ordeal, not least because it was painful to sit upright. The car seat was tilted back as far as it would go so that I was in a semi-prone position, but the seat belt pressed uncomfortably on the wound. The journey home was made bearable both by my sister's cheerfulness and good humour and by a stash of audio cassettes of Victoria Wood's screamingly funny TV shows. It really hurt to laugh, but I couldn't help myself. The cassettes kept me sane as we got snarled up in huge urban traffic jams in the less attractive parts of Belgium and France.

I cried with relief when we finally reached home and I saw my parents again. My operation had taken place on my mother's seventy-ninth birthday and I know that she and my father had been worried about me. Ten years on they are no longer alive and I miss them and think about them a great deal. We were always close-knit and loving and the day I returned home I was acutely aware of my good fortune in having such an affectionate, caring family.

Chapter 15

PILGRIMAGE
TO THE PIPS

AT THE BEGINNING of April 2008 an unprecedented event took place – most of the team of Radio 4 announcers and newsreaders were let loose in the East Sussex countryside to do a sponsored charity walk for the Lymphoma Association. This was because our much-loved friend and colleague, Rory Morrison, had been diagnosed with a rare form of blood cancer, Waldenstroem's macroglobulinaemia, four years earlier.

The event was called 'Pilgrimage to the Pips' because

we were heading to the home of the Greenwich time signal at Herstmonceaux Castle. The walk, which was about five or six miles in length and deemed acceptable to the more sedentary among us, was recorded to be broadcast as one of the *Ramblings* series of programmes later in April. Clare Balding, the award-winning presenter of *Ramblings* and the partner of one of our number, Alice Arnold, was there with her producer Lucy Lunt, preparing to walk with us and record our thoughts, both about the walk itself, our reasons for doing it and the unusual experience of being with our colleagues all day. For most of our time at work we hardly saw each other, owing to the nature of our shift system.

Friends and partners joined us for the walk, as well as representatives from the Lymphoma Association, and journalists from both *Ariel*, the in-house BBC magazine, and various specialist magazines dedicated to walking. We looked a fairly motley bunch as we gathered in a pub beforehand for coffee and biscuits. Every conceivable colour was worn and we all sported fleeces, waterproofs, walking boots and rucksacks; it was like an advert for Craghoppers. We were full of fun and laughter, anticipating a day of adventure free from the confines of a radio studio and the constraints of time, not least the tyranny of the pips marking every hour. Two dogs came with us – Peter Donaldson's Gully and Clare and Alice's Archie – who seemed to have a glorious time sniffing new and intriguing smells, and running and walking twice as far as the rest of us.

We had a group photo taken outside the pub in the sun-shine, although snow still lay thinly on the ground and surrounding hills and the wind had a biting edge to it. The trees for the most part were still bare, and glutinous mud trapped our boots as we squelched along deeply rutted tracks. The thing that made us truly happy that morning was that Rory was walking with us, along with his wife Nikki, and their children Honor and Reuben. He looked fit and strong and it was hard to believe that he had anything wrong with him, or had gone through some gruelling chemotherapy. We were delighted that he could be with us on our adventure.

As the walk progressed we fanned out over the coun-tryside, forming little groups that constantly changed to admit new people. We never seemed to stop talking or indeed laughing, gently mocking each other's efforts at climbing over stiles or remarking on how mud-spattered we had become. At one point we had stopped to make sure we were on the right track and a photo was taken. Some of us look, frankly, knackered, Rory is laughing – as he did all day – and yet more of us, naming no names, look as if we're on day release. Our boots and wellingtons are caked in mud, as are the lower halves of our trousers. One or two people look ready for their picnic lunch. I'd been walking happily arm in arm with Brian Perkins, whose gloriously deep voice graced the airwaves for sev-eral decades from the 1960s. We chatted about a myriad different things, often breaking off to launch into silly accents and then dissolve into laughter. At one point we were nearly up-ended crossing an exceptionally muddy field, our boots sucked into a swampy morass. Brian was one of my favourite announcers, both to listen to and to work with, and we always got on well. We invariably joked together and talked a lot about classical music, a shared interest. Before becoming an announcer, Brian had been a double bass player in the New Zealand Symphony Orchestra. I liked his attitude to life; he wasn't eaten up by ambition, but had got to the top of his profession, nonetheless, and was refreshingly free of ego. I have a natural aversion to those who constantly tell you how good they are and talk the loudest and longest.

I have a number of memories of that day: Diana resplendent in her grey beret, Zeb being a gentleman and offering a helping hand to those of us who were unable to vault over the stiles, and Lord Donaldson – as we called him – striding out in his red socks. (I hasten to add that he was not Radio 4's very own Naked Rambler – he was wearing other clothing!) Our group of announcers, the management of which had been described as 'like herding cats', came together for a common cause and to support Rory, a good and popular man. The spirit of unity and harmony was enhanced by the provision of whisky for all of us by a very kind newsroom colleague, Adrian Butcher, who lived in Sussex and joined us for the walk. The whisky was warming and sustaining and renewed our vigour. After a wee dram or three we positively skipped to our destination and got rather giggly and skittish.

Clare asked us how we imagined the Pips — for some they were an implacable foe, unforgiving and almost cruel. Others saw them as brightly coloured, furry little things that lived in a box. Alice had even seen them and said they had large ears.

By the time we all reached the pub at the end of the walk and settled down over drinks to review the day's events, everyone felt fitter than they had been at the start of the day and pleasantly tired. Clare had interviewed us all and — as ever — had done a highly professional job. The programme was broadcast at the end of April 2008 and got a very warm response, including some complimentary reviews. Most importantly of all, the Lymphoma Association received over £18,000 in donations. Pilgrimage to the Pips ended with Rory doing the closing announcement for the programme — he read it beautifully and we all cheered and whooped for joy. Rory was delighted and the rest of us — usually such a diverse and disparate group — basked in the glow of coming together and contributing to such a worthy cause. We all went home tired and happy, with some good memories of a rather special day.

It's six years since we undertook our 'Pilgrimage to the Pips' and Rory is no longer with us. He died in June 2013 having undergone a bone marrow transplant, but succumbing to a serious chest infection soon after. He was much loved within our group and is missed by all of us in different ways. I miss his laughter and humour and the way his face lit up when told something amusing or outrageous or both! He was a life-enhancer who certainly enriched my life; I find myself wishing he was around so that I could share gossip and jokes with him. When my mother died he came up to me and gave me a great bear hug; it was a simple and very human gesture, full of empathy and understanding. At that moment it meant far more to me than words.

A week after the first anniversary of Rory's death, Radio 4 held a memorial for him in the Radio Theatre at New Broadcasting House. His immediate and extended family were there and a number of the announcers and newsreaders shared their memories of Rory and the many funny stories about him that have passed into Radio 4 lore. Paddy O'Connell, the popular presenter of the programme *Broadcasting House*, acted as the master of ceremonies.

Rory's open, smiling face was projected onto a large screen hanging over the stage and we heard his lovely voice again. He was almost a tangible presence, and I half-expected him to come bounding into the theatre, grinning broadly and full of his usual enthusiasm and gusto. The heartfelt, sincere memories shared by my friends and colleagues were incredibly moving. Steve, Zeb, Neil, Corrie, Alice and I all contributed to the occasion, our reminiscences creating a picture of a kind, funny, generous-hearted friend and colleague. Sandi Toksvig and Richard Clark, the head of the newsroom, talked about Rory's talents as a part of the *News Quiz* team and as a newsreader.

As I've mentioned earlier in the book, Rory played a heroic part in Jim Naughtie's unfortunate spoonerism on the *Today* programme, when he introduced the Culture Secretary, Jeremy Hunt, as 'Jeremy C**t'! Rory stepped into this dangerously anarchic situation with aplomb, reading the opening cue of the eight o'clock bulletin calmly and coolly, and was rewarded with a bottle of wine by Gwyneth Williams, the Controller of Radio 4.

I've just become the Patron of WMUK, the charity for those with Waldenstroem's macroglobulinaemia, the rare blood cancer that Rory had. It's a testing tonguetwister of a name, even for professional broadcasters, so you can see why it's called the pithier WMUK. The charity aims to raise funds for a Clinical Data Registry and to raise the profile of the disease. Dr Shirley D'Sa, a consultant haematologist at University College Hospital, London, runs a specialist WM clinic there. She met me for coffee in March and showed me round the very impressive facilities at the hospital. She was kind and empathetic – I'm sure she has an excellent relationship with her patients. When I left the unit I felt doubly thankful for my own health and fitness; good health is an incredibly precious gift and I've been guilty on occasions of taking it for granted. I walked down the street in bright sunshine, relishing the warmth on my skin. I thought of all the people inside receiving chemotherapy and how they would have loved to be free to leave and feel the sun on their faces. It's a chance to help the charity in as many ways as I can, but above all to keep Rory's memory alive. He was such a vital, lively man, with an engaging exuberance, that it's hard to believe he's gone. This is the perfect opportunity for all of us to remember him, while doing something practical to raise funds for essential research and to help those who are living with the disease. Rory, you were a top man. Thank you for all the shared laughter and fun.

Chapter 16

THE BEAUTIFUL
GAME

THE EVENING BEFORE I left the BBC, *Newsnight* broadcast a feature they had made about me, ranging over my 27-year career with Radio 4 presentation. It was jokey, benevolent and complimentary and it was a great honour to have such a tribute from television, given that I'd spent my working life in radio broadcasting. The feature covered – inevitably! – my propensity to get the giggles, the Shipping Forecast and my close association with it and the many and varied news stories I'd dealt with over the years. Part of the feature consisted of an interview in which I was asked whether I had any unfulfilled ambitions. I said I would love to have read the football results as that had been a childhood ambition. I would sit, aged about six, at the kitchen table reading them out and studying the league tables very closely to see where my team, Spurs, were standing. My obsession with football was a big joke in my family – I used to ask for football annuals or a Spurs shirt and scarf as presents and read every football magazine that was available. My favourites were *Football Monthly* and *Shoot*. My ambition at that age was either to be a petrol pump attendant – I loved the smell! – or the first female centre-forward to play for Spurs. I was tall and strong and indulged myself in little fantasies that I would burst through defences or rise high above the other players to score spectacular volleys or headers. The goals were always sensational, never boring tap-ins or toe-pokes. I used to play in the park with my two friends, Robert and Anthony, and, like my tennis-playing, I was enthusiastic rather than notably talented! I would return home, my favourite red jeans spattered in mud, to tell my mother that I'd had a wonderful time. I remember feeling sad that I couldn't play football at school and was restricted to netball and lacrosse, neither of which lit my imagination particularly.

As a child, I read avidly about managers such as Ben Nicholson, Bill Shankly and Bertie Mee and soon learned the colours of every team strip in the First Division.

At one stage I could recite the names of the first team squads of all the London teams, and would write them down in an exercise book along with answers to football quizzes. This book once got handed in at school by mistake instead of my Latin homework, resulting in a very frosty exchange with my form teacher, who berated me for wasting time on trivialities. I was tempted to quote Bill Shankly's famous dictum that football was much more important than life or death, but thought better of it. I sometimes posed for family photos with a football, like my heroes in the football magazines. One year I asked for shin-pads as a birthday present.

I was fascinated by goalkeepers and their feats of agility; they could win or lose a game for their team and the weight of responsibility on their shoulders was enormous. Gordon Banks was a particular favourite; I marvelled at his extraordinarily quick reactions when making that legendary save from Pelé in the Mexico World Cup in 1970. I remember feeling saddened when he lost an eye in a car accident and had to give up playing. Another goalie I liked to watch was Peter Bonetti, whose lithe athleticism was always a pleasure to see. My favourite goalkeeper, however, was Pat Jennings of Spurs. He was a tall, softly spoken man from Northern Ireland, and had a modest, unassuming manner. He was a brilliant shot-stopper and was blessed with courage; he would often throw himself at the feet of an oncoming striker, risking injury to his head and body. I was fascinated by his enormous hands, encased in bulky, padded gloves. Rumour had it that his hands were the largest in the First Division; they were certainly adept at keeping a clean sheet for my team.

I have a romantic attitude towards football and love to see a small, cash-strapped team do well against a large, wealthy club in the FA Cup. Giant-killing escapades are always exciting – the plucky underdogs giving their all in a lung-bursting display against a superior, sophisticated side guilty of complacency. It's always sad to see a club with a noble history tumble out of the Football League altogether – Bristol Rovers suffering that fate in the 2013/14 season. I'm not keen on clubs that are bought by excessively wealthy owners, who in turn buy a ready-made team of expensive players from all over the world. I remain to be convinced that the players' first loyalty is to the club. As mad about the game as I am, I think that £250,000 per week is an obscene amount of money to be paid for playing football. The ordinary fan will never be able to earn that type of salary and often struggles to afford a season ticket. It's as if the biggest, wealthiest clubs are thumbing their noses at their most loyal supporters.

The bloated excesses and corruption of FIFA are equally distasteful; the venality of FIFA's officials is astounding. Sepp Blatter, the President of FIFA, seems to lack any insight or understanding, blithely contending that FIFA is a force for good in the world. He seems blind to the glaring fact that the organisation he presides over has lost all integrity and has become a byword for corruption and dishonesty. It's telling that he was not allowed to speak during the opening ceremony of the 2014 World Cup in Brazil, for fear of an angry response.

Against this tawdry background of FIFA greed and amorality and the extremes of vast wealth and deep poverty in Brazil, I was feeling a little jaded and cynical about the World Cup. The match between Spain and the Netherlands, however, restored my faith in the beautiful game. The Netherlands soundly beat the holders, Spain, five goals to one – an extraordinary result that I certainly hadn't predicted. It was sweet revenge for the Dutch after they were beaten by Spain in the World Cup final in 2010. The match featured two wonder goals by Robin van Persie and Arjen Robben, and yet again I found myself wishing that England had two players of comparable brilliance and skill. I love the excitement of a game like that, as the momentum takes play sweeping from one end of the pitch to the other. There was great talent on display, electrifying speed and memorable goals.

The World Cup semi-final between Brazil and Germany was extraordinary; I don't think anyone could have predicted how comprehensively Brazil would fall apart. Germany were clinical in their finishing, lethally fast in attack and very, very dangerous. Brazil's defence on this showing wouldn't have looked out of place in a Sunday League match. The final result, 7–1 to Germany, although an astonishing score-line, was an accurate reflection of the game.

I thoroughly enjoyed the World Cup final between Argentina and Germany, which Germany won 1–0 in extra time. The match wasn't the exuberant goal-fest of Germany's superlative semi-final win over Brazil, but the German team deserved to win. The German Wunderkind Mario Goetze showed great technique in capturing the ball on his chest and then volleying past the Argentinian goalkeeper, Romero. This was definitely a winning goal worthy of a World Cup final. Schweinsteiger was also magnificent at the heart of the German team and Neuer was a tower of strength in goal; the whole team believed in themselves. What a stark contrast with England – here the relationship between the FA and the Premier League is a mess and therefore we've got a national team that we deserve: twentieth in the FIFA world rankings, below Bosnia and Herzegovina, and unable to win a match in the group games of the 2014 World Cup. The future does not look rosy and may even get worse – how very, very sad.

Six months after I'd left the BBC I was rung up by Paul Blakely, the Deputy Controller of Radio 5 Live, and asked if I would like to read the football results, as James Alexander Gordon, a broadcasting legend who had done the job for forty years, was standing down. Paul and I had had many fascinating football conversations when he worked at Radio 4, so he was aware of my great love for the game and that I knew what I was talking

about. I replied without hesitation that he was pushing
at an open door and that I would love to do it. Apparently someone from the sports department had seen the
Newsnight interview and stored away my remark about
the football results. When James, who was universally
known as JAG, announced he was giving up, this man –
whose name I still don't know – told Richard Burgess,
the Head of Sport, about me. I am very grateful that he
remembered what I had said, as it has enabled me to ful-
fil my childhood dream.

A meeting was quickly arranged with Richard and
Audrey Adams; she had worked with JAG and was to be
my producer. Over coffee we talked about *Sports Report*
and the excitement of Saturday afternoons as the results
came in. We also discussed JAG and his immense contribution spanning forty years; he's a lovely man and I was
very sorry that he was having to give up through illness.
I liked Richard and Audrey a lot and knew immediately
that I would be very happy working with them. After
coffee we went to one of the small workshop studios in
New Broadcasting House and I read a few results. Richard and Audrey were both happy and that was it – I was
to succeed JAG as the reader of the classified results on
Sports Report on Radio 5 Live, the first woman to do so
on the BBC. I went home excited and delighted, marvelling at how extraordinary it was that life had come full
circle and I was about to do for real what my six-year-
old self could only dream about.

When the news broke at the beginning of August 2013, I was unprepared for the intense media scrutiny that followed. I had thought that the news would be of interest only to diehard football fans, but every news outlet seemed to pick it up and comment on it. Fortunately for me the reaction was overwhelmingly positive, although there were inevitable comments from a few unenlightened men who couldn't believe that a woman was capable of doing the job. My friends and family were thrilled as they knew I'd been besotted from a young age and that this opportunity was something that I would relish. I did an interview with Mark Pougatch for Radio 5 Live; Mark is a fine sports journalist and also very pleasant, so I felt comfortable chatting to him. He was intrigued to discover that my father was an Arsenal fan! I told him that my allegiance to Spurs wasn't an act of defiance, but more a desire to follow a team who played with flair and style. I also loved their distinctive name. My father, who was full of fun, gentle and kind, was tickled pink that I'd chosen to support Spurs and did no more than tease me when results weren't going our way.

A few weeks after it was announced that I would be the new reader of the classified football results, I was approached by the British Library and asked if I would record the thirteen original rules of football for an exhibition they were about to put on. It was to be their first ever football display, to mark the 150th anniversary of the Football Association (FA).

The centrepiece was the original 1863 FA minute book, valued at £2.5 million. The book contains the thirteen original rules and documents the historically important meetings of the newly formed FA. It also records the establishment of the world's oldest cup competition, the FA Cup, as well as the organisation of the first international football match. The book was compiled by Ebenezer Cobb Morley and is handwritten in a beautiful copperplate script. When I went to the British Library to do the recording I was allowed to hold the book and turn its pages. I felt very fortunate to be able to hold the most significant book in the history of football in my hands – and I didn't even have to wear protective white gloves! The book provides a fascinating glimpse into the origins of the nation's most popular sport.

Interestingly, the original rules stated that 'no player shall carry the ball' – the goalkeeper position didn't even exist in the early days of the sport. Another rule stated that 'neither tripping nor hacking shall be allowed and no player shall use his hands to hold or push his adversary'. Having watched a large number of the 2014 World Cup matches, that particular law seems to be utterly disregarded. The final rule stipulates that 'no player shall wear projecting nails, iron plates or gutta percha on the soles or heels of his boots'. The thought of projecting nails tearing into the muscle and sinew of a player as they attempted a tackle is truly stomach-churning. I also had to look up 'gutta percha' in the dictionary as I'd never heard of the term before – it's a waterproof substance like rubber, but harder. Golf balls in the nineteenth century, apparently, were made of solid gutta percha. All this detail made me think of the huge, cumbersome boots the early players wore and the alarmingly heavy, laced footballs they played with. I was always amused by the voluminous, flapping shorts they all wore; old footage shows that any fast running down the wing was achieved in spite of yards of loose material wrapping itself around the player's legs. The kit and equipment were definitely a hindrance and a far cry from today's ultra-sophisticated, lightweight gear. I'm just glad that projecting nails never played a part in boot design.

I did my first live broadcast for Radio 5 Live on 28 September, having been on holiday and busy with other commitments since the start of the season. The media interest started again and I tried as far as possible to go into purdah and keep a very low profile. I was acutely aware that large numbers of people would be listening, including those who wouldn't normally choose to tune in. I was determined to do a competent, professional job and demonstrate that I was capable of meeting the challenge. The *Sports Report* team were incredibly welcoming and I was really touched by their warm supportive texts in the days running up to my debut. Richard, Mark and John Murray all sent me lovely messages, while Eleanor Oldroyd and Jackie Oakley tweeted their support. I was particularly touched because these people were highly professional broadcasters whose work I both admired and derived great pleasure from. The icing on the cake was a very kind and thoughtful email from JAG himself, who wished me all the best and told me to 'make it your own'. It is advice that I have taken to heart; you have to be completely yourself on air and plough your own furrow. Otherwise it sounds horribly fake. 'To thine own self be true' is a maxim I've always tried to live by. Something else that heartened me was an article by Marina Hyde in *The Guardian*. She is a journalist who I've long admired both on the sports pages and in the main newspaper. She writes beautifully and is also very funny; hers is the name I always look for when I open the paper. I was thrilled to discover that she'd written about my appointment. True to form, it was witty and cogent – and above all, complimentary.

I'd done a reasonably good job of keeping the nerves at bay in the week running up to my first broadcast, but didn't sleep well the night before. When I woke up, I did some meditation and relaxation and felt better; I knew that once I'd got the first session out of the way it would never seem so nerve-racking again. Nor would the media interest be so great. As time ticked by before I had to leave the house, I deliberately tried to empty my mind of anything football-related. I read some poetry by John Donne – one of my favourite poets – and 'William and the Policeman's Helmet' from *Sweet William* by Richmal Crompton. They make strange bedfellows, but never fail to calm me down when I feel stressed.

At four o'clock I was in the small workshop-studio
with Audrey and facing another mini-ordeal: publicity photographs with a press photographer who turned
out to be an Arsenal fan! Posing for photos was the last
thing I wanted to do at that point, but dutifully spent fifteen minutes smiling, pointing at the Radio 5 Live logo
and pretending to read a script. When I look at the photos now I appear happy and relaxed, but inside I was
thinking 'I want this to stop'! In the event I had plenty
of time to sit quietly and prepare myself. At two minutes to five my heartbeat picked up noticeably and by
the time the signature tune started it was really pounding. Astronauts' heartbeats rise alarmingly in the few
seconds before lift-off. I'm not comparing my experience to that of an astronaut bound for outer space, but
it would be interesting to know what my pulse rate was
in the moments before starting.

An extraordinary thing happened when I actually
began – a calmness descended on me as the professional
training kicked in. I did the reading to the best of my ability and even began to enjoy it. The five minutes it took
to read the results sped by and when I reached the final
result I felt positively exultant and keen to do it all over
again – which is in fact exactly what I had to do for the
World Service.

At 5.20 p.m. I emerged from my bubble of fierce
concentration and felt an overwhelming sense of relief,
coupled with an equally overwhelming desire for a large

glass of Sauvignon blanc! My mobile wouldn't stop ring-ing and I received lots of lovely texts from my friends and family. Richard Burgess sent me a text to say how well I'd done. I went home in a bit of a daze, allowed myself that glass of wine and promptly fell asleep on the sofa. When I woke it was time for supper and I had a chance to talk about the experience. I was delighted on two counts: first that it was over and would never be quite so fraught again; and secondly that I'd given a good account of myself. I slept soundly that night and woke to some very favourable reviews in the papers. I now wanted to be left alone to get on with the job and not be the centre of attention.

Fortunately that is exactly how it has turned out. Audrey and I meet every Saturday afternoon in the workshop studio, make a cup of tea and discuss the latest happenings in *The Archers*. This is usually done with a mixture of fondness and exasperation, as is our discussion about our respective football teams, Watford and Spurs. There's also much animated chat about the afternoon's scores and who is moving up and down the league tables. It's a very enjoyable routine and we work well together. It is also pleasing to be able to return to New Broadcasting House every week to see old friends and colleagues in the newsroom. The real pleasure lies in knowing that I'm not tied to a rigid and unforgiving shift pattern, nor beholden to any authority figure. Late shifts and early starts are a dim memory and it's a wonderfully liberating feeling.

Before doing the interview with Mark for Radio 5 Live, I was filmed for a small slot on *Football Focus*, predicting that week's results in the Premier League. Points were awarded for guessing the right results and the correct score-line. Mark ran through the fixtures and I offered what I thought would be the likely results. I was really keen not to screw it up and come out with no points whatsoever. In the event I acquitted myself reasonably well and got nine points, which at the end of the season put me in joint third position with the Camp Bastion troops. Not bad for a girl!

There's something magical about the names of the teams in the Highland League and I particularly enjoy reading them out when the clubs take part in the early stages of the Scottish Cup. They share some of the same mysterious allure as the Shipping Forecast areas and trip just as pleasingly off the tongue – Brora Rangers, Buckie Thistle, Clachnacuddin, Strathspey Thistle and the altogether less romantic Inverurie Loco Works and Forres Mechanics. I found myself wondering what their grounds look like and whether they have a backdrop of rolling hills covered with heather. I also wonder how many people support them and whether the numbers attending drop in the middle of winter, when it's raw and dark and the rain teems down.

The Corbett Sports Welsh League also boasts some interesting names such as Afan Lido, Gap Connah's Quay, Bala Town, the New Saints and the more prosaic

Airbus UK Broughton. The other name that caught my eye was Rhyl, simply because the team didn't score for some weeks and I had to read out the slightly surreal words 'Rhyl nil'! Oddly enough I mentioned this to a friend, and the very next week they started to score again.

The 2014 World Cup was a wonderful diversion for a committed football follower like me, easing the withdrawal symptoms that emerge during the close season and providing plenty of spectacle to sustain me before the start of the new. Roll on Saturday afternoons at five o'clock, *Sports Report*, and its somewhat old-fashioned but evocative theme music, 'Out of the Blue'.

Chapter 17

LEAVING THE BBC

I MADE UP my mind to leave Radio 4 in the summer of 2012. Two voluntary redundancies were on offer and I'd become frustrated at having to turn down interesting work that would have stretched me, because of the somewhat limiting terms of my BBC contract. Another important factor was the shift pattern and the number of early starts and late finishes I was having to work. I'd been working irregular shifts since the age of twenty-two – and now at the age of fifty-six I felt I'd done my fair share and it was time to stop working such antisocial hours. I was like a boxer who'd fought too many fights and was in danger of becoming punch-drunk. After a shift on the *Today* programme I would look like a bruised peach and realised that it was time to break away. I wanted to spread my wings, not have them clipped. Increasingly I felt that the job had stopped being fun. The people I was closest to had, for the most part, retired, left or moved on; my great ally, Laurie, had very sadly died. The decision to leave was remarkably easy to make, although inevitably tinged with sadness. Such lengthy service – thirty-four years in all since leaving university – qualified me for BBC 'lifer' status. I'm wary of this sobriquet because it implies that you've become institutionalised and reluctant to step away from the all-encompassing embrace of the BBC. In fact, I felt very forcefully that I wanted to start anew and in the process refresh myself professionally.

The public response to the news that I was going to leave was overwhelming and gratifying. Articles and blogs were written and tweets sent that were generous in spirit and very complimentary. It was akin to being able to read my own obituary – and so self-affirming to learn that people respected and liked me, professionally and personally. A leader in the *Daily Telegraph* headlined 'Losing our Voice' even asked 'How can she be redundant when the whole country is devoted to her?' A flattering but probably inaccurate assertion. It went on to say that my voice was a benefit to the nation's health, quoting an article from the *British Journal of General Practice* in which a doctor had written that my voice was 'like being tucked up in bed with a hot-water bottle'.

After this initial flurry of reaction my life returned to relative normality and I was glad to dive under the radar again. I'm a private person and feel uncomfortable when the spotlight picks me out. I did do an interview with Eddie Mair on *PM* because I'm very fond of him, but that was the exception. One day, not long after the hullabaloo, an email popped into my inbox from Sam Jackson, the managing editor of Classic FM. He wrote that he'd like to see me to discuss new opportunities and we arranged to meet. Sam is delightful – bright and energetic, brimming with ideas and very funny. I got on with him immediately, as I do with anyone who makes me laugh. I liked the programme ideas that Sam was proposing and told him that I would be very happy to join Classic FM.

It was the perfect fit for me. Classical music has been an integral part of my life since childhood and continues to give me enormous pleasure. My parents took my sister and me to special concerts for young children when we were small. I was fascinated by the different instruments and excited by the sound the whole orchestra made. I have never lost that excitement. My father would bring along some pear drops and aniseed balls to have as a treat after the concert had ended. I soon learned that if I said I was bored during the interval I got an extra sweet; I wasn't remotely bored, but felt it was worth fibbing about in order to indulge my sweet tooth. Fifty years later I still experience a Proustian moment when I occasionally buy pear drops, the sugary taste saturating my mouth and instantly taking me back to my childhood, sitting on a seat in the Royal Festival Hall with legs dangling, transfixed by the sound of the brass section in Benjamin Britten's *Young Person's Guide to the Orchestra*.

I began at Classic FM at the beginning of April 2013, presenting my own programme, *Charlotte Green's Great Composers*, a two-hour show every Sunday afternoon focusing on composers as diverse as Bach, Ravel and Gershwin. There was a strong biographical element to the programmes; the key moments of the composer's life were highlighted with lengthy musical illustrations from major – and sometimes lesser-known – works. They were fun to do and I looked forward to going in to record them with my producer Jamie. I was also learning a lot myself. We would make a mug of tea and talk football before concentrating on Brahms or Schubert. Jamie is an Arsenal supporter, so there would usually be a rueful analysis on my part of why Spurs hadn't been as successful as their north London rivals. I enjoyed the relaxed, friendly atmosphere at Classic FM and the leisurely schedule – such a welcome contrast to the relentless shift pattern at the BBC. I felt so much more relaxed, less edgy and free from the dictates of the clock. Crucially, I was now my own boss and – with the help of an excellent agent – could decide what I did and didn't want to work on. It was bliss not to be subject to the petty irritations of office politics. I was also managing to sleep well, something that hadn't been possible when tied to an unforgiving shift pattern.

So, 2013 was becoming a charmed year for me. While happy and stimulated at work I also enjoyed some very pleasurable spin-offs. In March I learned that I had been voted Radio Broadcaster of the Year by the Broadcasting Press Guild, and was completely thrilled. It meant a great deal to me to be honoured in this way. The awards lunch was held at One Whitehall Place in the splendid Gladstone Library; the building was originally the home of the National Liberal Club, founded by William Gladstone. The 30,000 books in the library are replicas, but it is an impressive room with high ceilings and lots of natural light. The food and wine were excellent and I spent an enjoyable time talking to the other people on my table and listening to a series of witty acceptance speeches from, among others, Benedict Cumberbatch, Rebecca Hall and Olivia Colman. When it was my turn I gave a short, jokey speech (less is always more I feel) and am now the proud possessor of an attractive glass trophy, etched with my name, the date and the award I won.

In May 2013 I was invited to lunch with Her Majesty's Judges at the Old Bailey. This was a wonderfully traditional affair with the judges dressed in their wigs and gowns. We had a very welcome glass of champagne before going in to eat; while talking to them I learned that most of them were great fans of *The News Quiz*!

They were charming, erudite and humane; the tabloid stereotype of elderly, out-of-touch buffoons is a gross misrepresentation. The judges who sat near me at the long table were astute, funny and quick to laugh and I found their company immensely stimulating. One of them told me about his twelve-year-old daughter, who had said to him that he really shouldn't be rude to her because she would be paying his nursing-home fees before very long! After the lunch I was invited to sit in on a case that had reached an interesting point; it involved the murder of a teenage youth who'd been stabbed to death. The breadth of detail – some of it quite arcane – that had been mastered by both the defence and the prosecution was astonishing. Two things remain in my mind – the alarming CCTV footage and the expressions on the faces of the defendants. They were bored and uninterested and seemed to have given up on life as they sat slumped in their chairs. They were only in their late teens, but already their lives were limited, offering no prospect of fulfilment.

The news that I was to become the first woman reader of the classified football results on the BBC coincided with a lunch with some of my Radio 4 friends and colleagues. We had decided to meet to remember Rory (Morrison) who had very sadly died nearly two months before. He was much loved and there was a large gap at the table where he should have been. We sat outside on the pavement in a street close to New Broadcasting House

and raised a glass or three to Rory. The mood was convivial, in spite of the street turning into a wind tunnel as
the weather changed. There was much fond reminiscence,
gossip and laughter, typical of many Radio 4 gatherings.

I've also been glad to support the charity Practical
Action, founded by the author of *Small is Beautiful*,
E. F. Schumacher. They are an international development agency working with poor communities to help
them choose and use technology to improve their lives
today and for the future. I'm impressed with their aims
and the invaluable work they do in challenging poverty
in Africa, Latin America and South Asia. Last August
I recorded a Radio 4 Appeal for them that brought in
£20,000, and have also recorded a voiceover for a television advertising campaign and an interview for their
website. Wherever I go, and with each new person I
meet, the conversation – more often than not – turns to
football. Practical Action is no exception. Andy North,
who I first met at Broadcasting House when recording
the Radio 4 appeal, is a Coventry City fan. When we met
again, for the website interview, we got so engrossed in
discussing our respective teams and the state of the game,
we were both horribly late for subsequent appointments.

For the past three years, I have taken part in the Adfam
Charity's Christmas Carol Concert, in the beautiful setting of St Bride's, Fleet Street. I was originally invited
by Sandi Toksvig, who was then the Patron; she has now
handed over to Eddie Mair, so there is a strong Radio 4

connection. Adfam have been providing support for families affected by drugs and alcohol since 1984. Each year a group of actors and broadcasters read poems written by the parents, siblings or children of those affected by drug and alcohol addiction. These poems are deeply affecting and depict, often with haunting intensity, the great difficulty and heartbreak of living with an addict. Last year I met the parents of a girl who had died, at the age of just twenty, from an addiction to hard drugs. The pain was still apparent in the way they spoke about their loss. I admire the hard work that these charities do in helping vulnerable people, often unsung and with scant financial resources. It sometimes makes me feel that the job I do is essentially frivolous.

Chapter 18

PEOPLE AND PLACES

I WAS VERY fortunate to have had both my parents in my life until I was well into middle age. It still felt strange however, to be an orphan at the age of fifty-five. They were no longer the roof over my head; I was now exposed to the elements and there was no shelter from the storms. I couldn't go to them for advice any more or for loving support and solace.

My friendships mean a great deal to me and are an integral part of my life. Sometimes the simplest pleasures are the most enjoyable and I love to share a bottle of wine with friends and have a good a laugh at life's absurdities. Juliet is a particularly good friend who makes me laugh all the time, but we can also be serious together. She is funny, sensitive and thoughtful and I always look forward to seeing her. She doesn't take herself too seriously, which is something I particularly value, as I have an allergic reaction to people who bang on about themselves. We often meet in Hatchards and browse in there for a while – one of life's greatest pleasures – and then go out to lunch. My stomach always aches afterwards at having laughed so much. She can also deliver a devastatingly piercing whistle, a talent that I admire enormously; my own efforts are disappointingly pathetic!

Laughter is the connective tissue that links all my friendships – I couldn't be close to someone who didn't possess a sense of humour. Mine is ribald and I love wordplay, puns and double entendres. My friends bring out the best – or is it the worst? – in me in that regard. Some of the evenings we have spent at a favourite Indian restaurant in Soho have been legendary, and we've all nearly ended up under the table as the wine has flowed and the laughter has grown louder.

My friend Tim has a very impressive modern art collection covering every available space on his walls; it's a real treat to wander round his house studying them and I've learned a lot from him. We both share a love of classical music and often discuss composers, musicians and favourite recordings. Tim is a true subversive who questions authority and believes in holding senior managers to account. I find his attitudes refreshing and the days spent alongside him in the newsroom were fun and amusing. It was cathartic verbally to skewer various irritating middle managers and indulge in a jokey rant about their heavy-handed style.

My friends are very different and that in itself is a pleasure; I love their diversity and distinctiveness. Many of my friendships involve lunch or dinner and trips to the cinema and theatre. I enjoy discussing current affairs, feminism and sport, among many other subjects. One friend used to be a doctor but is now a successful artist; she has a very good sense of humour and is always up for a laugh. I love her work and bought a beautiful oil painting at an exhibition she held in Aldeburgh in June 2013 during the festival. She is synaesthetic and paints her response to the work of Benjamin Britten, in this case his opera *Gloriana*, which last year celebrated sixty years since its first staging. The colours are strong and bold and I often just sit and stare at it, absorbing its vividness. It gives me particular pleasure to own a picture that's been painted by a friend.

I first met my friend Jan in the early 1980s when we were both studio managers and doing shifts in the Norman Shaw building near Parliament. The day's proceedings were recorded in their entirety, so we were forever loading up the tape machines with new spools of recording tape and labelling the old ones with the date and time. I can still recall the peculiar smell when the brand new spool was taken out of its box and plastic covering. We also had to record interviews between the parliamentary correspondents and sundry MPs who walked over to the studios from the Commons. Some were testy and impatient, others relaxed and genial, while a select few were so obnoxious that a collective groan went up when we were told that we would soon be blessed with their presence. My favourite memory is of our lovely studio cleaner, who always brought in cakes and biscuits for us to have with our tea. She was no respecter of people or reputations and on this occasion marched into the studio mid-interview, blithely ignoring the red light indicating that a recording was taking place, and started to hoover. The studio guest was even asked to lift his feet so that the hoover could reach under the table. The bemused expression on his face was a glory to behold, irritation and frustration battling it out with good manners and a desire not to lose his temper. The cleaner was eventually ushered out of the studio and asked by the producer to respect the red light. We then started again, but none of us could really concentrate as we were still chuckling over 'Hoovergate'.

Jan and I loved incidents like that, revelling in their absurdity. I soon learned she liked to laugh as much as I did and had an equal dislike of pomposity and stuffed-shirt tendencies. We also shared a keen interest in the theatre and of course, music, so often went to the theatre and concerts together. Because of the nature of

our respective shift patterns we used to book for mat-
inees and would joke about being surrounded by a sea
of grey hair, the high-pitched squeal of malfunctioning
hearing-aids and a murmur of disapproval if a rude word
was uttered on stage. With the unthinking cruelty of the
young who think they'll never grow old, we christened
them the Croydon Day Care Centre Group. It won't be
long before I qualify to join them!

The pleasing thing about our friendship is that we
immediately pick up the threads whenever we haven't
seen each other for a while – Jan has now moved out of
London to a beautiful area on the English–Welsh border. We slip easily into laughter and jokiness, knowing
exactly who and what makes the other one laugh; neither
of us feels the need to try to be something that we're not,
so it's immensely relaxing to be in each other's company.

When I was working full-time at the BBC I relished
the buzz and excitement of a busy newsroom, but needed
peace and quiet as essential antidotes to the endless noise
and commotion at work. It's important for me to be able
to relax and have time just to be, and live in the moment.
It's why I enjoy walking so much – it provides physical exercise, a chance to immerse myself in the beauty
of the landscape and escape into the solitude of remote
places. Scotland provides all this for me; I love to walk
in Perthshire, where the sheer beauty of the colours, the
hills and the heather provide enormous solace and give
me the chance to shrug off any stress or worry. A walk

in this magnificent landscape is like a form of meditation, a chance to refresh and revive myself.

Perthshire was also where my aunt lived. I had only
one aunt (as opposed to aunts by marriage) and Margaret
was the best sort – interested in what Rachel and I were
up to, always supportive and encouraging and the dis-
penser of wise advice about our respective careers. She
wasn't, however, particularly interested in very young
children – I remember at the age of about four being
rather hurt when she told me not to get my sticky fingers on her blouse! Once we were older she was always
pleased if we rang her up to discuss a particular issue.
She was my father's younger sister and looked up to him,
as most younger siblings do. She had once allowed him
to entwine a little clockwork car in her hair; it got so
deeply entangled that a section of her hair had to be cut
off. As a teenager during the Second World War, she was
evacuated to an army general's home in Cheltenham and
always maintained that this experience was the making
of her. Margaret had been a shy child, but the general
encouraged her to discuss current affairs and form her
own opinions. She gained self-confidence and grew up
into an extremely able and intrepid woman who travelled all over the world.

Margaret was good at sports and won a Blue for net-
ball while a student at Oxford. She read classics at St
Anne's College, but the experience was rather surreal.
Most of the male students had been called up, and the

female students were expected to do a certain amount of war work alongside their studies, including knitting socks for soldiers. Margaret was always ready to have a go and decided to canoe through the rain water sewer under the centre of Oxford with a friend. This was quite a risky escapade – if it had rained while they were in the sewer they could well have drowned.

Earlier Margaret had taught classics and theology at a girls' school in Bristol, and every August ran an outward bound-style house party for girls. I joined the house party once or twice. I loved the long walks and climbing we did in the local hills. Whenever I visited Margaret and her husband in Pitlochry we always walked up Ben y Vrackie or to Loch Ordie, a beautiful hidden loch surrounded by hills. They remain two of my favourite walks, redolent with memories of my aunt.

Margaret and I would discuss any subject while we walked – music, literature, politics or the magnificent Scottish landscape. They were happy times and I remember them fondly. When she grew frail and moved into a nursing home, my sister and I would visit her in Pitlochry and remember all the walks we had done together. The last time we were able to take her out in her wheelchair, we took her to the Queen's View, a spectacular viewpoint over Loch Tummel with the mighty mountain Schiehallion in the background. We'd been there many times as children and had also climbed Schiehallion on a number of occasions. She loved it and I'm so glad we were able to take her there one last time. She opened up all sorts of vistas for me, but I'm particularly grateful that she introduced me to the delights of walking in the unsurpassed beauty of the Scottish countryside.

I also love to walk in Dorset, a beautiful gentle county, brilliantly evoked by one of my favourite authors, Thomas Hardy. The Hardy Society have produced a series of walks that plot a route through the landscapes so memorably drawn by him. I know his novels well, so it adds an extra dimension to walk through the countryside where Hardy set *The Woodlanders*, or the lush fertile Vale of Blackmore that provides the backdrop to *Tess of the d'Urbervilles*. I'm fortunate that a friend of mine lives in Dorset and I'm able to roam through his own woodland with his gorgeous black Labrador, Bess. It's fascinating to see the landscape in different seasons – it's almost impossible to imagine that the woods, so black and bleak and bare on New Year's Eve, will burst forth into a profusion of bright, newly minted foliage and fat sticky buds in the spring.

Walking is my main physical relaxation. I love the sense of space, the fresh air and the small, subtle changes in the hedgerows and trees each time I venture out. The physical exercise stretches my long back and legs, which sometimes feel stiff and cramped after a long session in the recording studio. Two longish walks on a Dorset holiday, shortly after I left the BBC, remain a golden memory and took place on two near-perfect days. We walked from

Povington Hill to Lulworth Cove and then walked back again; low winter sunlight washed the hills around us. Out to sea the water glistened and gently lapped against the cliffs. As I walked I made a mental note to remember the views, the quality of light and the – occasional – joy of physical exertion. I say occasional because at one point in the walk the cliffs became very steep and we had to drop right down to sea level and then tackle a vertiginous climb. The effort wasn't made any easier by a strong wind buffeting us as we climbed, doing its utmost to push us off the cliff and into the sea. Progress was quite slow; short pauses to get my breath back were disguised as map-reading and a reflective scanning of the horizon! Humiliatingly, just at the toughest part of the climb, two teenage boys shot past with the surefootedness of gazelles and the enviable stamina of the young and very fit. They greeted us cheerily – fortunately I had enough puff left to respond without sounding as if someone was standing on my windpipe. The boys sped on and I resumed my stately climb to the top, where I was rewarded with magnificent views across the sea and the sight of plump clouds scudding towards the horizon.

Once at the top and on level ground we virtually skipped along until we made the descent into Lulworth Cove. I was famished by now so we headed for a pub and ate a gorgeous crab sandwich. The walk back was equally invigorating and just as tough when we dipped down into the valley and started the long climb. There was nobody else around by this stage; the winter sun was casting very long shadows and the two of us were like tiny ants dwarfed by a vast landscape. It was exhilarating reaching the top again and seeing the magnificent view open up, like a gift presented to us by nature as a reward for our efforts. We made it back to Povington Hill as dusk descended and the light gradually drained away. We were walking in a monochrome world, a stark counterpoint to the vivid colour earlier in the afternoon. But what a day – physical effort, great natural beauty and the sheer exultation of being active and alive.

Two days later we were lucky enough to experience the same glorious golden light as we walked over Swyre Head, the highest point in the Purbeck Hills, to Kimmeridge Bay and back, one of my favourite walks. There was utter peace apart from the natural sounds of birdsong and the distant boom of the sea. The clarity of the light enhanced the spectacular views along the Jurassic Coast. It was uplifting to be part of that landscape on such a glorious day.

Good friends of mine live in a small hamlet in Suffolk, not far from Aldeburgh and Southwold. I really like walking in the wide, open spaces that surround their home. Every time I go I stare at the immensity of the sky and clouds; it feels liberating and is such a contrast to the grey lowering sky over London that squats on your shoulders. Their fox terrier is a friendly little soul who's always keen to go for a walk; it's rejuvenating to trudge through the fields and watch her run as fast as her little legs will go, chasing an elusive scent. I've also fallen in love with Aldeburgh – quirky, quaint and colourful with its slightly eccentric inhabitants, excellent bookshop and atmospheric shingle beach. It's a place redolent of Benjamin Britten and his extraordinary creative output. One of the most enjoyable short walks I've done encompassed a visit to the Red House, where Britten lived with his partner, the tenor Peter Pears, and a walk along Aldeburgh beach to Maggi Hambling's strikingly beautiful steel sculpture *Scallop*, dedicated to Benjamin Britten. It's wonderfully invigorating exercise, especially when the wind is blowing and the waves are big and powerful.

In London, I love the changing seasons in Kew Gardens, particularly springtime. Seeing the brand new foliage and its vivid, fresh colour is balm for the soul, as are the startlingly bright colours of the azaleas and roses. I like the immutable quality of the trees, standing upright for 200 years or more, established long before I was born and likely to be still standing long after my allotted span is up. It gives me pleasure to think that they will grace the gardens for at least another hundred years, their stark beauty in winter and canopied glory in spring and summer bringing delight to future generations. I also enjoy the more rugged beauty of Richmond Park, but Kew Gardens holds my heart. As a child I used to be bored walking there with my family, wandering along morosely a few feet behind the others, scuffing the toes of my shoes and hoping that we could soon go home. I seemed to be oblivious to the beauty, caught up in my own inner preoccupations. Now, I fully understand why my parents loved it so much; my appreciation of beauty in all its forms increases immeasurably the older I get.

Although I'm gregarious with friends and love the chance to meet and socialise, I'm also quite happy spending time on my own, pottering about in the garden or immersing myself in a book. Music is an essential part of my life. London, although infuriating at times and impossibly overcrowded, noisy and rude, nevertheless offers an astounding choice of excellent cultural events, ranging across theatre, music, film and dance. As a Londoner, I'm spoilt for choice every night of the week. I thought about becoming an actress when I was young and did a lot of drama at school, but as I grew older reality took hold and I realised that I would spend a lot of time resting in between roles! I also suffered from pre-performance nerves before school and student productions, which didn't augur well for a future career. Almost to the very end of my career at the BBC, I would get nervous backstage before *News Quiz* recordings at the Radio Theatre. I'd pace up and down in the moments before going on, trying to cultivate an attitude of creative indifference. As soon as I went on stage it would all evaporate and I would be fine – I'd relax into the whole occasion and usually have a great time, but the nerves were an unwanted distraction.

Some of my happiest and most transformative experiences have occurred in the theatre and the concert hall. I find it genuinely exciting to watch live theatre and see work of the highest quality; I'm often moved to tears or laughter by a powerful performance. As a small child I almost wet myself, such was my excited anticipation of *The Wind in the Willows*. Nowadays my bladder control is excellent, but the excitement remains just as acute! The actors I particularly love to see perform are Dame Judi Dench, Simon Russell Beale, Fiona Shaw, Juliet Stevenson and Alex Jennings. I feel the same electrifying expectation when watching musicians perform live, especially soloists such as Mitsuko Uchida, Anne-Sophie Mutter and Andras Schiff. I like to spend time on the South Bank at the Royal Festival Hall and the National Theatre and often go to the Wigmore Hall, which has an authentic middle-European feel to it. I'm lucky to be able to go to Glyndebourne every year, which on a warm summer's evening is breathtakingly beautiful and magical. The combination of the luminous Sussex countryside, the sheep grazing on the other side of the ha-ha, and the first-class music-making is unbeatable.

Sometimes the most enjoyable experiences are unforeseen and take you completely by surprise. Philippa Stanton, the actor and artist, got in touch to ask if she could paint my voice. She was doing a series of similar paintings for an exhibition in Brighton and asked if I would agree to meet her. It sounded fun and innovative so

I said yes immediately and we arranged to meet in London. Philippa is very lively and warm, and infectiously enthusiastic about her work. She is also synaesthetic, and sees colours when she hears voices. The predominant colour in my picture was a beautiful pale purple, like the colour of wisteria, which happens to be one of my favourite plants. I have a well-established one in my garden, which looks glorious every spring. Philippa also added white oil paint to represent what she kindly said was the creaminess of my voice. It's an abstract work but there's a movement and shape to it that looks like a wave about to break on the shore. When I saw it I fell in love with it and promptly bought it. It was exhibited in Brighton and now hangs on my wall. Earlier in my career a listener asked for a publicity photo and a fortnight later sent me a lovely watercolour, taken from the photograph. I was surprised and delighted, especially as it was obviously a labour of love. Recently, a small caricature of me appeared in *The Guardian* in the birthdays column. I liked it so much that I contacted the artist, Nicola Jennings, to ask if I could buy it. She agreed and the original A4-size work now also hangs on a wall at home.

I grew very fond of the work of the artist Valerie Thornton, the internationally recognised etcher and print-maker. I originally bought one of her etchings from the Royal Academy Summer Exhibition, which depicted Pulteney Bridge in Bath. The RA send your details to the artist when you buy a picture and they then contact you. She wrote me a very sweet letter asking if I was the Charlotte Green on Radio 4, whom she listened to while working. I replied that I was and she told me she was delighted I was buying one of her works. She was very interested in architecture and I went on to buy a number of her etchings of church interiors; two favourites are *Lincoln Cathedral Choir* and *St Ethelbert's Gate, Norwich*. I make my mind up very quickly when I see a work of art that I want to buy. Valerie's work leapt out from the wall and I'm delighted that I've been able to continue to collect her art – in spite of her death in 1991. Her etchings have a beautiful stillness about them that appeals to me greatly.

Out of the blue I was asked to write a chapter on how to give a talk, as a contribution to a book published by the *British Medical Journal*, *How to Present at Meetings*. George Hall, professor of anaesthesia at St George's, University of London, wrote to me to say he was editing the book and, having heard me on Radio 4, hoped I would like to contribute. I wrote a section on controlling nerves while giving a talk or lecture and gave a slightly frivolous piece of advice – if your audience seems a little daunting as you stand before them, imagine them all naked. Nudity is a great leveller! That piece of advice was given to me when I was about to embark on a series of university interviews and stood me in good stead, although at times it was slightly distracting.

Since leaving the BBC and going freelance, I have

had the opportunity to meet and interview some of the most interesting and creative actors, musicians and writers working in Britain today. Interestingly, I have not so far felt daunted interviewing them, nor have I needed to take my own advice and imagine them naked, in order to allay any potential nerves!

Chapter 19

2013 AND BEYOND

IN SEPTEMBER 2013 I began a new project at Classic FM and
I now present an Arts and Culture Show on the network,
Charlotte Green's Culture Club, in which I interview well-
known musicians, actors, writers and comedy performers.
Creative people invariably have fascinating stories to tell and
express themselves well; it's stimulating work and stretches
me professionally. Classic FM is a relatively small set-up
compared to the mammoth operation at the BBC, but very
inclusive and friendly. I was made welcome from my
very first day. Presenters often refer to fellow presenters'
programmes on air and the style is relaxed and hospitable.

At Christmas I went for a seasonal drink with my fellow presenter Anne-Marie Minhall, my producer Jenny and my former producer Jamie, who worked with me on my *Great Composers* series. It was a very convivial time and we made the most of the opportunity to relax. Anne-Marie and I stayed on after the other two had gone back to work and got stuck into the mulled wine, which was particularly good. After a while we decided to have one last glass, only to discover that we had drunk the pub dry of their mulled wine supplies. To be fair we weren't the only people in the pub drinking it, but we'd probably made considerable inroads. Neither of us was due to be in front of a microphone that afternoon and I have a very strict rule that I never drink alcohol while working. It's far too easy to assume that one drink won't make a difference, but it does; the microphone is a very unforgiving instrument in that regard.

My producer, Jenny, and I enjoy our trips away from Global Towers (as we call the Classic FM building) to interview film stars such as Sir Roger Moore, well known for his urbane charm. He went out of his way to ensure that I was comfortable and had everything I needed. Sir Roger has a lovely, self-deprecating sense of humour and described his work as no more than being able to avoid bumping into the furniture! I liked him very much and Jenny and I went away utterly charmed by him. For one morning only I'd got to play the role of Bond Girl, albeit one who was rather long in the tooth!

I particularly enjoyed going to the home of the distinguished conductor Sir Neville Marriner, to interview him as part of Classic FM's 'Marriner at 90' celebrations. He is an extraordinary force of nature and could easily be taken for a man twenty years younger. His son Andrew, the principal clarinettist with the London Symphony Orchestra, was also there. They regaled me with some excellent stories about working together and the funnier aspects of being on tour. They are both very talented musicians at the top of their profession, yet I was struck by their humility and lack of arrogance. I imagine they would be great fun to make music with, while also setting very high standards of professionalism. The Academy of St Martin in the Fields, established by Sir Neville in the late 1950s, is a world-class ensemble with a very distinctive, beautifully precise style of playing. My parents loved their music-making and so I was very fortunate to hear them play a lot when I was growing up. As the interview progressed, each of Sir Neville's collection of exquisite antique clocks struck the quarter-hour and half-hour with its own distinctive chime. It was as if the clocks wanted to show that they too could make music. At the end of the interview, Sir Neville kindly invited me to his concert celebrating his birthday with the Academy at the Royal Festival Hall. It was a memorable occasion with musicianship of the highest quality – I felt privileged to be there and hear music by Saint-Saëns, Mozart and Elgar played with such brio and verve.

I've admired the actor Emma Thompson ever since I saw her on television in *Fortunes of War*. I like the fact that she is down to earth and determined not to be starry – quite a difficult feat to pull off in the parallel universe of Hollywood. She's naturally funny and unafraid to be outspoken, so I was thrilled when I learned that I was to interview her. She came in with Celia Imrie, another actor who has great comic timing and charm. It wasn't so much an interview as a laugh-in; both of them are effortlessly funny and made me laugh so much that I had stomach-ache by the end of the session. I loved their larkiness and appreciated their commitment to the interview, in spite of a punishing publicity schedule. At no point did they move onto automatic pilot. Emma Thompson has moved me to tears on a number of occasions, most notably as Miss Kenton, the emotionally repressed housekeeper in the film *The Remains of the Day*, and the Harvard University professor in *Wit*, who is diagnosed with ovarian cancer. This latter role is, I think, one of her finest pieces of work. Her intelligence shines through her acting and I feel lucky that I've been able to see her in the theatre and on film performing at her peak.

Fiona Shaw is another acting hero of mine whose performances are electrifying. She is mesmerising to watch on stage and really compels your attention. I first saw her as Madame de Volanges in *Les Liaisons Dangereuses* in 1985 and have followed her career ever since. I liked her immediately when she came in to be interviewed; she had a friendly, direct manner and greeted me warmly. Refreshingly, she'd arrived on her bike and without any entourage. We began talking about her preparation for her role in *The Testament of Mary* by Colm Tóibín, for which she was about to start rehearsals at the Barbican. She's a deep thinker and gave a lot of consideration to the questions; she was also great fun and had a real twinkle in her eye. The time allotted to the interview shot by and reluctantly I had to wrap it up. I would love to have her back on the programme again for a more wide-ranging discussion. The Barbican subsequently gave me seats for *The Testament of Mary* and it was an astonishing tour de force, a performance of astounding power and intensity. At the end of the play she received a lengthy, thoroughly deserved standing ovation and the audience seemed reluctant to let her go. I think everyone was acutely aware that they'd just witnessed something very special.

Yet another highlight was the chance to interview Juliette Binoche, the immensely talented French film actress, artist and dancer – a true Renaissance woman. She's effortlessly stylish in a way that comes so naturally to French women. She was fascinating about the creative process and how she approaches her work; she also spoke eloquently in English. When she smiled her face lit up, full of imagination and intelligence; she completely charmed me and gave me an excellent interview. In her latest film, *Camille Claudel 1915*, she plays the title role with great passion. Claudel was the sculptor and lover of Auguste Rodin, but was incarcerated in an asylum in 1913 for the remaining years of her life. It's a serious and powerful film.

I was lucky to have Stephen Fry as my very first guest on the *Culture Club*. He can talk effortlessly on any subject, in an interesting and funny way. The time I spent with him was both fascinating and instructive. We were discussing Wagner, the man and his music, and I felt afterwards as if I'd had a particularly stimulating tutorial on the subject. Beforehand we'd both had to fight our way through hordes of One Direction fans in Leicester Square, who were waiting for the group to appear. It's sad that classical music doesn't – yet – generate that level of excitement in young people. Stephen hoped wistfully that the fans were there to see him, but at least he hadn't experienced my moment of mortification. As I pushed my way through to get into the building a girl of about fifteen turned to her friend and said, 'She can't be anything to do with it; she's much too old!' I hope that Stephen will appear on the programme again; his wit and charm make him the perfect guest.

An ambition of mine came true when I interviewed the magnificent soprano Jessye Norman. She is a genuine superstar and I felt a mixture of apprehension and excitement before meeting her. The evening before the interview I listened to a recording of her singing the *Four Last Songs* by Richard Strauss. He wrote beautiful music for the female voice and the *Four Last Songs* are haunting and evocative. Three of the songs are settings of poems by Hermann Hesse; they are an extraordinary mixture of tenderness, stillness and peace of mind. The song that concludes the cycle, 'Im Abendrot', is a setting of a poem by Eichendorff; it's very moving and depicts a contented leave-taking. Strauss was eighty-four when he composed the *Four Last Songs* and the work seems to describe his readiness for death. Jessye Norman sings the songs with a magnificent poignancy and subtlety; her voice is beautiful and moved me to tears.

When I met her she was charming and gracious. During the interview she spoke about her recently published memoir, *Stand Up Straight and Sing!*, and recalled her childhood in the segregated south of the USA and her time living and singing in Berlin, a divided city when she was there. As we spoke she described freedom as being of the utmost importance and told me about helping a talented East German opera singer to achieve her own freedom by defecting. When I asked her what advice she would give to an aspiring young singer, she replied that everyone should be ready to work and prepare, and be willing to enjoy the preparation process. As she rightly said, working hard is its own reward.

The interview with Jessye Norman has definitely been one of the highlights of my time at Classic FM. She's a very impressive woman with great dignity and presence; in spite of her status as a true superstar of the opera world, she came across as very interested in other people and willing to give a lot back. She founded the Jessye Norman School of the Arts in 2003, a tuition-free performing arts after-school programme for economically disadvantaged students in Augusta, Georgia, and spoke warmly about how the students gained a great deal in learning how to express themselves and acquire self-esteem. I'm thrilled I've met her and was able to thank her for all the pleasure her singing had given me.

I could not be happier in my relatively new role and relish the chance to see a lot of theatre, hear a lot of music and watch new films. I also enjoy the preparation for my interviews as well as the interviews themselves. Jenny, my producer, and I generally agree about the people we meet and our response to them – only one was deemed to be a bit of a bore!

I've mentioned in an earlier chapter that I received an honorary doctorate from the University of Kent in 2013. The university celebrates its fiftieth anniversary in 2015 and I look forward to joining them in marking this milestone. Six months after the honorary degree ceremony I spent a lovely afternoon in late April on the campus, having been invited back to open the university's state-of-the-art new Media Centre. I was given a very warm welcome and was particularly struck by the enthusiasm and commitment of the students. The afternoon passed in a blur of interviews for both radio and television, recording station idents and posing for selfies with the students! The day ended with a delicious meal in Canterbury with the Deputy Vice Chancellor and the Director of Development and Alumni Relations.

The year ended with the news that I was to be inducted into the Radio Academy Hall of Fame. It was lovely to be recognised and honoured in this way by fellow professionals in the industry and I'm very proud to be keeping company with some very distinguished radio broadcasters. At Christmas I went through my diary as an aide-memoire to some of the special moments that had taken place since I left the BBC. My holiday in Dorset stands out because I remember it as a time of great happiness. I was excited about the future and starting work with Classic FM; it felt as if anything was possible and life was truly exhilarating again.

Chapter 20

STEPPING INTO
THE FUTURE

WHEN I WAS much younger a few friends and I would joke at work about eventually living in a Home for Retired Newsreaders and Announcers. We'd all be arrayed around the four walls of the living room, each in our own separate world of memory and reminiscence. As we sat there we would open imaginary faders and speak into an imaginary microphone, muttering the well-worn phrases 'This is Radio 4' and 'In a moment, *The World At One*'. It seemed funny at the time, especially as we gilded the lily by adding made-up programme titles such as 'Running Sores' for 'You and Yours' or 'A BLOODY Good Read' instead of the more restrained *A Good Read*. And those are the printable ones! Peter Donaldson would always refer to *Day News* as 'Day Snooze' and *Today* was sometimes referred to as 'Toady'.

I would occasionally worry once I'd decided to leave the BBC that I would miss the work too much and regret my decision. This hasn't happened and it's proved a remarkably easy transition to move from the BBC to freelance work. I still retain a great affection for the BBC and a good number of the people who worked there, but it's been a boon to gain a fresh perspective on life and to strike out on a different path, doing exciting work and meeting new and stimulating people.

In order to finish this book I stayed in a lovely cottage in the midst of an arable farm in Herefordshire, surrounded by magnificent views of the distant Brecon Beacons, while in the foreground lay huge fields of waving barley fringed by old-established oak trees. The cottage was a converted forge, very comfortable and cosy with pale pink roses tapping at the window in the breeze.

One evening I went for a walk round the perimeter of the farm, to the site of an old Iron Age fort, the mound covered in the pale and dark green foliage of a huge variety of trees, like a painting by the English artist and etcher S. R. Badmin. The day had seen heavy showers, but by mid-evening there was a glorious golden light offset by the inky blue of the sky and scudding clouds. It looked as if some rain might fall, but the golden hue prevailed and bathed the landscape of patchwork fields in a gorgeous gentle wash. The only sounds were the murmur of the breeze in the leaves and occasional birdsong, as a few swallows swooped overhead. It was peaceful and calming, the perfect counterpoint to a busy day; the exercise felt good as my walking boots crunched over stones and splashed through muddy puddles created by the rain earlier in the day. I was reluctant to end the walk and headed back to the cottage only when the light began to fade.

As I grow older, I hope the memory of this walk – and others like it in Dorset, Cornwall, Suffolk and Scotland – will sustain me. Similarly, my memories of a happy career in broadcasting and the laughter and friendships it has brought me. I've been very fortunate to have had such fun in both my work and my personal life – and I will certainly keep on laughing!

ACKNOWLEDGEMENTS

I WANT TO say a big thank you to Richard Anthony Baker for planting in my mind the idea of writing a book, and for introducing me to my charming and excellent literary agent, Robert Smith. Robert's support and helpful suggestions have been invaluable.

I've really enjoyed getting to know the delightful team at The Robson Press, particularly Olivia Beattie and Victoria Godden, both of whom have been so supportive and encouraging. Many thanks too to Jeremy Robson for agreeing to publish the book and for his charm, courtesy and warm welcome. Suzanne Sangster, Katy Scholes and James Stephens have all worked hard on my behalf and I'm very grateful.

I'd like to thank my friends for their excitement about the project and want to say a huge thank you to my sister Rachel. She has been unfailingly helpful and encouraging throughout the writing of this book. Her memories of our shared childhood gave me fresh insights into our early life, and her laughter, when reading certain passages that I had written, spurred me on. It would have been so much harder without her.

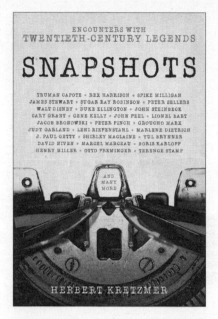

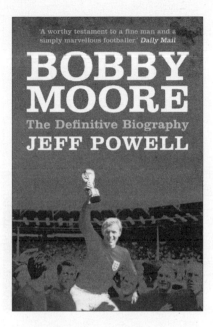